THE ANATOMY
OF LITERATURE

THE ANATOMY
OF LITERATURE

BY

HAROLD R. WALLEY

ASSOCIATE PROFESSOR OF ENGLISH

AND

J. HAROLD WILSON

ASSISTANT PROFESSOR OF ENGLISH
THE OHIO STATE UNIVERSITY

FARRAR & RINEHART

ON MURRAY HILL   NEW YORK

To

ERMA AND LOUISE

I have only this of Macrobius to say of myself, *Omne meum, nihil meum,* 'tis all mine and none mine. . . . We can say nothing but what hath been said, the composition and method is ours only and shows a scholar . . . yet I say with Didacus Stella, "A dwarf standing on the shoulders of a giant may see farther than a giant himself."

—*The Anatomy of Melancholy*

PREFACE

The Anatomy of Literature is not a history of literature. It is not a criticism nor a study of critical theory. Nor yet is it another book designed to arouse the reluctant student to what is known as an appreciation of literature. Its purpose is quite humble and not in the least spectacular; it might even be said to be entirely practical. Its purpose is simply to present in compendious form such information as the average intelligent reader should possess in order to understand what literature is, of what it is composed, and what it is trying to do. In other words, it is concerned with those cells, tissues, and members which go to make up the artistic body which is known as literature. For that reason the book has been called advisedly an anatomy.

The present book is based upon certain convictions which should be understood at the outset. In the first place, the authors have little faith in an appreciation of literature which is not founded upon understanding. Admittedly understanding does not insure a vital appreciation, but appreciation divorced from understanding is likely to be a pallid flower of uncertain growth. In the second place, the authors are equally convinced that a resolute exposition of literary technique as such in the classroom is perhaps the most expeditious method of smothering whatever interest in literature the student may

have. It is a dull business for the teacher and an indigest-
ible one for the student. Moreover, even if insisted upon
by a Spartan, though misguided, zeal, the result is rarely
encouraging. Students have a way of misunderstanding
even the most lucid explanations and of perpetuating such
mistakes in their notebooks. Even when the notebook is
reasonably accurate, the lapse of amplifying memory often
leads to subsequent error. The attempt to remedy this
deficiency has led the authors to a final conviction: that
there is an astonishing dearth of books which, without
involving the student in minutiæ of detail and abstruse
discussions for which he is ill prepared, present, con-
veniently and simply, enough of the basic facts about
literature as an art to prepare him for an intelligent appreciation and love.

The Anatomy of Literature is an attempt to meet this
need. It does not pose as the final word on literary technique, theory, and criticism. It is intended as a convenient
reference book for the student. On the other hand, it is
not merely a haphazard and undigested accumulation of
irrelevant facts. Literature is viewed throughout as an
art, and the book is an attempted rationale of what constitutes that art. True, the authors have not striven for
originality; nevertheless the book is the result of independent investigation and represents an endeavor to produce a reasoned synthesis of the rather nebulous and
often illogical materials of literary discussion. Inevitably
it has often been necessary to cut Gordian knots with
apparent dogmatic abandon. The authors have been compelled only too often to rush in where even archangels

may fear to tread. Nevertheless they have made haste
slowly, preferring to sacrifice, when need arose, minute
accuracy for the sake of clarity and fundamental truth.
After all, in matters literary one is never likely to speak
from the pinnacle of absolute truth. Under the circumstances, partial knowledge, if it be clearly comprehensible
and not mischievously misleading, is preferable, at least
for the beginner, to a confusing labyrinth which may or
may not eventually lead to perfect understanding. Some
few pronouncements involve matters of literary dispute
wherein, even at best, the discussion has been more speculative than judicial. Rather than suppress them in silence,
the authors crave for their own conclusions the same
tolerance which must be granted all those who set themselves to the serious and conscientious elucidation of artistic problems.

Mechanically the book is designed for practical convenience. Everything, we hope, which an intelligent reader
should know about the mechanism of literature is discussed at one place or another in the book. In the simplest
language possible is explained the nature of each subject, its use and purpose, its artistic value, and its place
in the whole technique. Illustrations, wherever possible,
have been chosen from literature with which the student
may have some familiarity. If the book is read from
beginning to end, the student will be presented with a
logical unfolding of literary art designed to lead him
from general considerations to matters of technical detail. In order are discussed the nature of literature, its
general kinds and purposes, the materials of which it is

constructed, its various intellectual and emotional attitudes, the general mechanics whereby it becomes articu-
late, and finally the important types and forms of literature with their specialized technique. But the book is also
designed as a convenient reference book. The index will
locate readily any subject desired, and all important subjects in the text are set off typographically. An analytical
outline of the contents emphasizes the logical unity of the
whole subject and at a glance relates the mechanical detail to the whole artistic structure.

The Anatomy of Literature has grown out of the needs
of the authors and many of their colleagues and students.
It is intended to be no more than an humble, if rather
necessary, handmaid to that finer appreciation and love
of literature, the stimulation of which is the ambition of
every teacher. If it may be found useful to that end, the
labor of its authors and their immeasurable debt to a host
of critics, colleagues, and friends will be abundantly
justified.

H. R. W.
J. H. W.

Columbus, Ohio,
    April, 1934

TABLE OF CONTENTS

TO THE READER

The acquisition of a love for literature is in many ways like the contraction of a disease. It may arise from environmental conditions. It may be the result of sheer chance. Often it is contagious, and one may not be certain exactly how it has been caught. But, unlike many diseases, it is not to be induced by simple inoculation. One does not come to love literature merely by making up one's mind, nor by submitting to the ministrations of others.

Similarly an appreciation of literature is not to be achieved through mere good intention or the earnest efforts of well-meaning instructors. True, one may catch some of the enthusiasm of an able guide; one may concede the beauty and significance of that which he obligingly points out. And in time one may come to acquire something of the taste which informs him. But enthusiasm alone, or even enjoyment, is not the same as appreciation. Of course, one may always pretend; and of pretence about literature there is only too much. One need but recall the passing fads and the retreating procession of each season's literary lions to recognize how much of literary acclaim is dictated by fashion or amiable blindness rather than by informed judgment.

Nevertheless the difference between the genuine and the spurious appreciation of literature is as apparent as

it is great. To the true lover, literature is not merely a
social amenity, a trivial pastime, a convenient escape from
tedium or inconvenience; to him it is life itself, life articu-
late, thrilling, and inexhaustibly beautiful. It is the en-
veloping atmosphere wherein he has his being—as immediate, as necessary, as practical as the food and drink
with which he nourishes his body. For the lover of literature there is no need to argue the value of its art. He
knows that the art of literature is integral to that supreme
art, the art of living. For him literature is life distilled
to wisdom, at once a question, a synthesis, and a con-
summation.

The simple truth is that both an appreciation and a
love of literature are twin plants of a quite natural, if
not almost unconscious, growth. Much depends upon the
soil from which they spring. With care and cultivation
growth may be promoted artificially. But also the seed
may fall by chance and the plant grow wild. One thing
alone is needful if the plant is to flourish and be sturdy:
that the root of the plant be firm. And that root—the
foundation of all intelligent appreciation and love of
literature—is understanding.

Let us pause a moment. The word "appreciate" literally
means to set a price or value upon something. But obviously the only appraisal of value which is worth anyone's
consideration is one which springs from a sound understanding of that which is appraised. The perils of mere
casual judgment are sufficiently set forth in Franklin's
familiar story of the costly whistle. One youthful experience was enough to convince that hard-headed sage

literature is to be appreciated as a work of art. The same general conception may be expressed by the essayist, the novelist, or the lyric poet; but each will interpret it in his own way and present it according to the peculiar technique of his special art. Obviously, then, one must be able to distinguish and understand the technical language which an author speaks if one is to comprehend what he says.

But in addition to its usefulness as a practical aid to understanding, a knowledge of literary technique has an æsthetic value in itself. In almost every activity of life which includes the application of skill, the initiate is capable of a more intense enjoyment than the neophyte. It is those who have mastered the technique of dancing or of tennis who derive the most positive pleasure from them. Even the mere observer knows the artistic delight which comes from seeing a thing done properly and well. It is not uncommon to speak of a beautiful tackle on the gridiron, or of a beautiful double play on the diamond, or of a beautifully played hand at the bridge table. In such cases one is not employing words loosely; one is speaking with entire exactitude. A beautiful tackle *is* beautiful in a strict, æsthetic sense. One is simply paying tribute to the artistry of a thing done artistically.

There are many ways of attempting an effect, and as a rule most of them may succeed after a fashion. But ideally there is one best way which, with economy of means and energy, achieves the desired effect easily, directly, smoothly, and gracefully. The selection and employment of that best way is what is meant by artistic technique. The perfect adjustment of appropriate means to desired end is a large part of what is meant by beauty. There is a definite æsthetic joy which springs from a recognition of the goal aimed at and of the skillful art which moves surely and beautifully to the attainment of that goal. Such is the secret of literary appreciation. The more one knows of its elaborate technique, the better qualified one is to extend the resources of one's enjoyment and to enter into the authentic thrill of artistic attainment which makes literature for the initiated a thing of beauty and a joy forever.

But art, unfortunately, is long and time distinctly fleeting. Moreover, for the average intelligent reader it is neither necessary nor desirable that literature be made a dull complexity of mechanical detail. Certain fundamental knowledge of the art of literature is an essential part of sound culture; the rest may be left to the specialized study of the practicing artist. It is the purpose of the present book to assemble such basic knowledge, to digest it, and to explain its meaning and purpose as simply and as clearly as possible.

ANALYTICAL OUTLINE

THE ANATOMY
OF LITERATURE

CHAPTER I

THE NATURE, PURPOSE, AND CONTENT OF LITERATURE

The word literature is derived ultimately from the Latin word *littera,* meaning letter. In its derivative sense it means simply anything which is written or printed. Usage, however, has tended to restrict its meaning to such written or printed matter as repays the reading by virtue of its subject matter or its style. Usage further recognizes two general kinds of literature: non-creative literature, and creative literature.

Non-creative literature is simply a written record of facts. Its principal value is its subject matter. Qualities of style are unessential, and exist merely as gratuitous embellishment. And as the chief virtue of that subject matter is its accuracy, the only contribution of the writer which has any consequence is his knowledge of the subject and his veracity. In this classification may be included such writings as news stories, source books, most text books, dictionaries, and encyclopedias, as well as many scientific reports on journeys, explorations, and investigations.

Creative literature, on the other hand, is the product of a writer's selection of, and imaginative building upon, facts. It is, as the term implies, a new creation, bearing the stamp of the writer's individuality. Now this stamp of individuality is composed of many qualities, but for the sake of convenience they may be considered as belonging to two categories. To the first of these may be given the name vision, and to the second the name style.

By vision is meant the writer's view of life and the interpretation which he gives to whatever falls within that view. The creative writer is an artist. As an artist he views life as the raw material of art. In human experience he seeks some order or design which will impart to it beauty and meaning. Failing to discover such a pattern, he may endeavor to impose upon life some pattern of his own making. But in either case what is finally expressed in a work of creative literature is the artist's vision of life interpreted in the terms of his own personality. This interpretation, which in a work of literature may often be reduced to an abstract conception or idea, is what is technically known as the **theme** of the literary composition.

But, as we have said, creative literature is an art, and the stamp of individuality which it bears is the stamp of a creative artist. It is not merely that literature expresses the interpretation of life by an artist, but that the interpretation receives expression at the hands of an artist. For it is in the expression itself that the personality of the artist becomes manifest. It may be the writer's attitude toward his material which reveals his personality, or it may be his little mannerisms of expression. But much more it is his distinctive craftsmanship which reveals the artist, in the pattern he imposes upon his material and in the methods he employs to achieve his desired effect. It is this combination of qualities which is meant by the term **style.**

Literature in its creative, or restricted, sense is an art, and as such implies considerable skill in the making. Centuries of literary experiment have refined upon that skill until now such literature possesses a highly specialized artistic technique. It is with this technique that the present book deals. Since non-creative literature is not an art, and thus possesses no specialized technique, it requires no special discussion. Therefore it should be understood that the kind of literature discussed throughout this book is creative literature, literature viewed as an art.

As a form of art, then, literature may be defined as a verbal interpretation of life by an artist.

The purpose of literature, in general, since it is an art, is to give pleasure and profit to the reader. The kinds of pleasure and profit given by particular works of literature depend, of course, upon the specific purposes of the artist. These immediate purposes, however, naturally group themselves into two major classes, each associated with a corresponding classification of literature. To these latter classifications Thomas De Quincey in a famous essay gave the names, "the literature of knowledge," and "the literature of power." These names, while not necessarily definitive, may be accepted as convenient descriptive terms.

The purpose of the literature of knowledge is to develop in the reader an understanding of experience.

Such literature does not merely present facts; it interprets facts into a systematic and coherent order. This systematic interpretation is designed to produce in the reader knowledge, that is, the clear and certain understanding of truth. In other words, it attempts to develop in him the ability to perceive, to apprehend, to know. Such is the purpose of works like Darwin's *On the Origin of Species,* and Bryce's *American Commonwealth.*

The purpose of the literature of power is to develop in the reader an attitude toward experience. Although, in method, such literature too may work through the interpretation of facts, its purpose is to release potentialities within the reader, to exalt him, to enable him to see and feel more sharply, to live with a stronger sense of the richness of life. In short, it develops within him the impulse "to grasp this sorry scheme of things entire, . . . shatter it to bits—and then remould it nearer to the heart's desire." Such is the purpose of works like Emerson's *Essays,* Shakespeare's *Hamlet,* Whitman's *Song of Myself,* and Hardy's *The Return of the Native.*

Whatever may be the purpose of literature or the form in which it is cast, the actual content of literature may vary widely, independent of purpose or form. This content is of many kinds. Specifically, the kind depends upon two factors: the nature of the material chosen, and the attitude of the writer toward his material.

The material with which the writer works may be either found in the world about him or created in his own imagination. Both, of course, because of the limitations of the human mind, are ultimately based upon the phenomena of human experience. But in the first case the writer makes use of those materials which are admittedly, or can be proved to be, part of the sum total of human experience. For example, poetry like that of Burns, a novel like Sinclair Lewis's *Main Street,* a record of personal experience like Mark Twain's *Life on the Mississippi,* or a play like Ibsen's *The Pillars of Society,* are all based upon such material. In the second case the writer creates, by a readjustment of the raw materials of life according to a new and individualistic pattern, an imaginary world of his own. For example, Barrie's *Peter Pan,* Cabell's *Jurgen,* Swift's *Gulliver's Travels,* and Coleridge's *Rime of the Ancient Mariner,* are based upon this material of the imagination.

The second factor in determining the content of literature is the **attitude of the writer toward his material.** This attitude, since it depends upon innumerable elements of environment and personality, is, of course, unique with every writer. Nevertheless, the personal attitude of any writer is bound to include certain universal attitudes which can be recognized independently and defined. These universal attitudes are of two classes: those which represent, in effect, judgments of the ultimate value of life, and those which indicate preferences for certain optional values of life.

The first of these classes includes four recognizable **judicial attitudes:** optimism and pessimism, and sentimentalism and cynicism.

(1) *Optimism and Pessimism*

Optimism and pessimism are intellectual judgments of the value of life. Optimism is the reasoned conviction that the good in life outweighs the evil. Pessimism is the reasoned conviction that the evil in life outweighs the good. Thus Walt Whitman, seeing both evil and good, arrived at the optimistic conviction that life, despite the manifestations of evil, was fundamentally good; while Mark Twain, with much the same evidence to reason from, arrived at the pessimistic conviction that life, despite the manifestations of good, was fundamentally evil.

(2) *Sentimentalism and Cynicism*

Sentimentalism and cynicism are emotional, rather than intellectual, judgments of the ultimate value of life. By a process of rationalization they are made to masquerade as intellectual judgments. Sentimentalism is the emotional belief that there is good in everything, that evil is either negligible or non-existent. Cynicism is the emotional belief that everything is evil, that good does not exist, and that what appears to be good is merely evidence of naïveté or hypocrisy. Thus such writers as Richard Steele or Louisa M. Alcott, refusing to see the evil in life, clung to the sentimental belief that all life was good or could be made so, while such writers as Etherege and Rochester, refusing to see the good in life, adhered to the cynical belief that all life was evil and could not be improved.

The second class of universal attitudes contains three recognizable **preferential attitudes:** realism, romanticism, and classicism.

To define these latter attitudes with scientific precision is impossible because of the numerous variant meanings which they have collected during centuries of use. Different critics, from time to time, have defined the terms, each emphasizing that element which seemed to him predominant in the literature which he had under discussion. In defining romanticism, for example, Theodore Watts-Dunton called it "the renascence of wonder"; Sir Walter Raleigh saw it as chiefly "the magic of Distance"; while Walter Pater looked upon it as "strangeness added to beauty." For practical purposes, however, it is possible to describe these three major attitudes in terms of their constituent elements.

In general, realism and romanticism may be considered as two preferential attitudes toward life which represent opposed extremes. **Realism** is an attitude which endeavors to find truth through a submission to fact; **romanticism** seeks to find truth through an escape from fact. In other words, realism limits its interpretation of life to its scientific perceptions of fact; romanticism interprets life through an arrangement of facts in accordance with its intuitive conceptions.

[A specialized form of realism is known as *naturalism*. Whereas realism limits itself to the perceivable facts, naturalism emphasizes the scientific analysis of the factors, heredity and environment, and the biological processes whereby life becomes what it is.]

Whereas these two attitudes represent extremes, **classicism** is not an extreme; it is the golden mean between the two. Classicism neither succumbs to fact nor flees from it; classicism accepts facts in their just proportion and interprets them in accordance with a perspective of reasoned symmetry and perfection. It endeavors to "see life steadily and see it whole."

More particularly, the opposed attitudes of romanticism and realism may be described in terms of a number of well-known antithetical components. The more important of these are defined below.

(1) *Distance and Propinquity*

Romanticism tends to seek the strange and the remote; realism tends to prefer the familiar and the near. Thus, from the familiar routine of the commonplace, romanticism has sought escape to nature and "communion with her visible forms," to far-off lands "beyond the sunset and the baths of all the western stars," to dream worlds glimpsed through magic casements, to the future where "the world's great age begins anew," or to the past of "old, unhappy, far-off things, and battles long ago." Realism, on the other hand, has preferred the immediate in time and place. In its attitude toward nature it has been scientific rather than rhapsodic. Its interest has been "any streetful of people buying clothes and groceries, cheering a hero or throwing confetti and blowing tin horns."

(2) *Freedom and Determinism*

As romanticism desires escape from the uncongenial, so it tends to set up the positive ideal of freedom from uncongenial restraint; as realism submits to things as they are, so it tends to bow to their immutable laws. Thus romanticism is often characterized by a note of rebellion, political, social, or spiritual. On the other hand, realism is usually characterized by a note of graceful or grudging acquiescence to that which it feels is already determined by natural forces beyond human control.

(3) *Individualism and Universalism*

As romanticism sets up the positive ideal of personal freedom, so it tends toward individualism; as realism submits to law, so it tends toward universalism. Individualism is the exaltation of the individual above the mass as a self-sufficient realization of a universal plan. Universalism is the reduction of individuals to a common level upon which they appear as no more than biological phenomena.

(4) *Subjectivity and Objectivity*

As romanticism emphasizes the individual, so it tends toward subjectivity; as realism emphasizes the universal, so it tends toward objectivity. Subjectivity is the interpretation of life in terms of personal conviction. Objectivity is the interpretation of life in terms of impersonal conviction arrived at through experimental observation.

(5) *Deduction and Induction*

As romanticism is frequently subjective, so its reasoning tends to be deductive; as realism is frequently objective, so its reasoning tends to be inductive. Deduction is a process of reasoning from general principles to particular instances. Induction is a process of reasoning from particular instances (evidence) to general principles. Thus romanticism tends to present illustrations of an idea with little concern for their resemblance to actual life. Realism, on the other hand, tends to emphasize the accuracy of the evidence from which conclusions may be drawn.

(6) *Idealism and Materialism*

As romanticism usually reasons from fundamental principles, so it tends to be idealistic; as realism usually reasons from evidence, so it tends to be materialistic. Idealism is the belief that ultimate truth exists only in the realm of ideas; that is, that truth exists only in the form of mental or spiritual concepts. Thus romanticism tends to portray a world which resembles the ideals of perfection in the writer's mind, rather than ordinary experience. Materialism, on the other hand, is a belief that truth can have no existence apart from the realm of physical phenomena, and, therefore, man's knowledge of truth must forever be limited by his sense perceptions. Thus realism endeavors to portray a world which resembles ordinary experience; beyond this it refuses to go.

(7) *Mysticism and Scepticism*

As romanticism is usually idealistic, so it may tend toward mysticism; as realism is usually materialistic, so it may tend toward scepticism. Mysticism is the belief (1) that all existence, both physical and spiritual, is but a manifestation of one universal entity which may be known by a number of names, such as God, Brahma, Over Soul, Life Force, World Spirit, etc.; (2) that the supreme goal of life is to lose personal identity and become one with the Universal Being. Scepticism, on the contrary, is an attitude of doubt based upon the reflection that, since there is nothing beyond the world of experience, and since human knowledge is incomplete, nothing can be accepted as a final revelation of truth.

Classicism, as remarked before, differs from both romanticism and realism in that it does not represent an extreme. Nevertheless it must not be viewed as an attitude of compromise between irreconcilable extremes. It is rather a harmony of elements which it does not feel to be mutually exclusive.

Classicism does not see life as sharply divided into good or evil, true or false. It holds that there is no falsehood without its grain of truth, and that truth itself, if carried to an extreme, may become false through disproportionate emphasis. Its fundamental ideals are "the golden mean" and "nothing too much." Thus classicism sees all the elements of life as supplemental to each other, and seeks ultimate truth, beauty, and goodness only in a harmonious synthesis wherein each component performs its proper function.

From the foregoing it may be seen that the essence of classicism is harmony and proportion. Its ideals are balance and symmetry. Its concern is with totality rather than detail. Thus in both life and art its valuation of any part is guided by its consciousness of the whole. It avoids eccentricity and cultivates the normal and well-balanced. It tempers emotion with reason and exalts the intellect as the means of perceiving and controlling symmetry. It concentrates upon the human as the loftiest synthesis of the natural and the divine. Through the apparent chaos of experience it forever seeks order, law, design—the final pattern which reconciles truth with beauty and constitutes perfection.

Since certain of the outward characteristics of classicism can easily be recognized and isolated, they may readily be imitated. From time to time individuals or whole generations have admired the spirit of ancient Greece and, to a certain degree, of Rome as preserved in their classic literature and art, and have attempted to emulate it. Frequently this is done by imitating the classical principles of restraint, decorum, regularity, austerity, elegance, and intellectuality. Sometimes the result is the noble serenity of the ancient spirit, sometimes mere sterile adherence to rules. Such an imitative attitude, particularly of the latter sort, is frequently known as **neo-classicism.**

CHAPTER II

THE MECHANICS OF LITERATURE

The principal distinguishing characteristic of literature as an art is skilled craftsmanship or technique. This technique, gradually evolved over centuries of experimentation, consists of, first, the various mechanical devices and methods whereby the writer gives artistic expression to his conceptions; and, second, the structural pattern, or form, which the artist imposes upon his materials. To the first of these the present chapter is devoted. The artistic forms of literature are discussed in the remaining chapters.

The technical name for the mechanics of literary expression is rhetoric. Rhetorical technique is an integral part of both poetry and prose, its respective functions differing not in kind but merely in degree. Therefore what is said about the mechanics of literature must be understood to apply equally to prose and poetry.

[The ultimate difference between *prose* and *poetry* is largely one of content, intention, and manner. The distinction between *prose* and *verse,* on the other hand, is one of form—of the rhythmical patterns imposed upon language.]

Rhetorical technique, in so far as it is concerned with more than the mere rudiments of self-expression, is of two major kinds. The first is concerned with the mechanics of presentation; that is, with the devices and methods whereby the writer provides an artistic existence for his conceptions. The second is concerned with the mechanics of appeal; that is, with the devices and methods whereby the writer engages the co-operative interest of the reader and prompts a response to the challenge of his artistry.

I. Mechanics of Presentation

The methods by which the writer provides an artistic existence for his conceptions are generally grouped in the four divisions of description, narration, exposition, and argumentation. These divisions, of course, are not mutually exclusive; often one method may seem to be intruding upon the province of another. For example, scientific description and exposition can hardly be separated. Furthermore, in the making of a single work of literature, more than one method is commonly employed. Frequently all four are used to produce a blend so perfect that the reader is hardly aware of the underlying mechanical structure.

DESCRIPTION

Description is the portrayal of concrete objects by means of words. Its purposes are (1) to present the object to the reader with an air of verisimilitude, (2) to arouse in the reader by the portrayal of certain aspects of an object the emotions felt by the writer on seeing the object, or (3) to picture an object as the embodiment of an abstract concept in the mind of the writer.

The methods employed in achieving these purposes are known respectively as imitation, impressionism, and expressionism. Broadly speaking, the last two of these may be considered as first and second steps away from the superficial appearance of things, with which imitation alone is concerned.

Imitation is the descriptive method which endeavors to create an illusion of actual experience, whether its subject be drawn from the world of experience or from the world of the imagination. The artist, of course, may select only those details which he wishes to present, but his finished picture must have a totality of effect which agrees with the experience and knowledge of his readers. The result for the reader should approximate the result of actually seeing the object. Thus, the essence of imitation is the awareness of fact.

Imitation is the method most commonly employed in literature. For example, when Herman Melville, in *Typee,* wished to portray for the reader the habitation in which he spent so long a time in semi-captivity, he wrote as follows:

Near one side of the valley, and about midway up the ascent of a rather abrupt rise of ground waving with the richest verdure, a number of large stones were laid in successive courses, to the height of nearly eight feet, and disposed in such a manner that their level surface corresponded in shape with the habitation which was perched upon it. A narow space, however, was reserved in front of the dwelling, upon the summit of this pile of stone (called by the natives a "pi-pi"), which, being enclosed by a little pocket of canes, gave it somewhat the appearance of a verandah. The frame of the house was constructed of large bamboos planted up-right, and secured together at intervals by transverse stalks of the light wood of the hibiscus, lashed with thongs of bark. The rear of the tenement—built up with successive ranges of cocoa-nut boughs bound one upon another, with their leaflets cunningly woven together—inclined a little from the vertical, and extended from the extreme edge of the "pi-pi" to about twenty feet from its surface; whence the shelving roof—thatched with the long tapering leaves of the palmetto—sloped steeply off to within about five feet of the floor, leav-ing the eaves drooping with tassel-like appendages over the front of the habitation. This was constructed of light and elegant canes, in a kind of open screen work, tastefully deco-rated with bindings of variegated sinnate, which served to hold together its various parts. The sides of the house were similarly built, thus presenting three quarters for the circu-lation of the air, while the whole was impervious to the rain.

In length this picturesque building was perhaps twelve yards, while in breadth it could not have exceeded as many feet. So much for the exterior; which with its wire-like reed-twisted sides not a little reminded me of an immense aviary.

The imitative method of description used in literature, as has been seen, employs selected details and gives to each an arrangement and emphasis in proportion to its value in creating a total effect. The imitative method is also used for the descriptive purposes of science. When so used it is not concerned with the presentation of a total effect. Rather it gives an accurate picture of the thing, and of each detail in proportion to its value, for the pur-pose of complete knowledge rather than for the purpose of sensuous effect. This method is known as **scientific description.**

Impressionism is the descriptive method which attempts to convey to the reader only the impression made by an object on the artist's senses. It pictures those aspects of the object which will cause the initial impression to be reproduced upon the reader's senses. The impressionist seeks to picture the object not as it actually appears but as it seems to him at the moment when it affects his senses. The essence of impressionism is the awareness of feeling.

Thus Sherwood Anderson in his story *Out of Nowhere into Nothing* described a city in terms of the impression it made upon a young woman looking out upon it from an office window. She saw the sky, grey with smoke. It was late afternoon and she was impressed with the tremendousness of the city in the light of the falling sun. As she gazed westward the whole city began to reach upward. "It left the ground and ascended into the air. Stark grim factory chimneys, that all day were stiff formal things sticking up into the air and belching forth black smoke, were now slender upreaching pencils of light and wavering color." The chimneys detached themselves from the buildings and leaped upward. The girl felt herself being lifted, achieving an odd floating sensation. Even the chimney of the building in which she stood was leaping upward. "With what a stately tread the day went away over the city." And the city hungered after it.

Here, surely, is the awareness of feeling. The city itself is not pictured; rather the reader sees it through the eyes of the character, and the impression of sudden expansive movement felt within her is induced also within the reader.

This is the method of much modern painting, poetry, essay writing, and fiction. In the last it is particularly exemplified by such writers as Dorothy Richardson, James Joyce, May Sinclair, and Sherwood Anderson.

[Impressionism is a term also applied to a type of criticism which judges a work of art not according to definite standards but according to the impression which the work has made upon the critic. Such a critic, well exemplified by Walter Pater, has been defined as one who pursues "the adventures of his soul among masterpieces."]

Expressionism is the descriptive method which substitutes for the thing seen a symbol of what the thing means to the writer. It presents a spiritual world of abstract ideas embodied in forms. It makes no attempt to imitate the superficial appearance of things; it expresses the artist's conception of reality in pictures which give concrete realization to the abstract. Often these pictures are highly fantastic, and not infrequently they require of the reader or observer a considerable exercise of the imaginative powers to pierce through them to the abstractions of which they are the visible expression. The essence of expressionism is the realization of thought.

Expressionism in contemporary literature has received its fullest development in the theatre. Particularly notable examples are Rice's *The Adding Machine,* Kaufman and Connelly's *Beggar on Horseback,* and O'Neill's *The Emperor Jones.* Because of the scope of expressionism, however, it is hardly possible to illustrate it with a specific passage. Perhaps a brief analysis of the expressionistic method as employed in O'Neill's *The Emperor Jones* will serve the purpose. Here the author is interested in showing the breakdown of a civilized negro, Brutus Jones, under the impact of various intangible forces, chiefly his own recollections of his violent past, and the revived collective memory of the race to which he belongs. Attempting to escape from the wrath of his savage subjects, the Emperor Jones plunges into a primitive forest and is shown, in a series of successive scenes, wandering in circles deeper and deeper. His passage through the forest symbolizes his spiritual progress deeper into the forest of his own personality. Consequently, in each scene, symbolic expression is given to one of the forces within his personality which is reacting upon him to bring about his eventual downfall.

The first of these forces is symbolized as a group of "Little Formless Fears . . . black, shapeless," the second as an episode from his past, a crime he has committed, and the third as another episode from his past, a glimpse of his life as a member of a chain gang. Then the racial background begins to awaken, expressed, first, in a scene of pre-Civil War days, in which Jones is auctioned to the highest bidder, second, in a glimpse of Jones among the naked blacks on a slave ship, and, finally, symbolizing his complete reversion to the primitive, a scene in which the negro is subdued and hypnotized by a savage witch-doctor. Obviously, all these scenes are the embodiment of abstract concepts in forms which give visible expressions to the abstractions.

Yet it is not the author's intention that these scenes should be considered merely as dreams or nightmares; rather he shows them as a blending of two planes of reality, the actual and the mental. Jones actually does go through these horrible experiences, his hysterical mind projecting into the actual world about him the mental forces of which each scene is a visible representation.

NARRATION

Narration is the orderly account of an event or a series of events, real or imaginary. In artistic narration, as aids to the presentation of the material, two subordinate methods are used to supplement the straightforward account of the event. These methods are called direct discourse and indirect discourse.

Direct discourse is the method of representing the speeches and thoughts of characters directly, that is, dramatically, as if the reader actually heard the speech or thought. Usually, but not always, direct discourse is indicated in writing by the use of quotation marks. Two devices used for the presenting of speech and thought dramatically are dialogue and monologue.

Dialogue is a dramatic presentation of the give and take of conversation between two or more people. This is the most generally used method of direct discourse, as in the following example from Edgar Allan Poe's *The Gold Bug:*

"Did you say it was a dead limb, Jupiter?" cried Legrand in a quavering voice.

"Yes, massa, him dead as de door-nail—done up for sartain—done departed dis here life."

"What in the name of heaven shall I do?" asked Legrand, seemingly in the greatest distress.

"Do!" said I, glad of an opportunity to interpose a word, "why, come home and go to bed. Come now!—that's a fine fellow. It's getting late, and, besides, you remember your promise."

Monologue is a dramatic presentation of the speeches or thoughts of a single character. Strictly speaking, the orator, the radio or vaudeville speaker, the lecturer, or anyone who speaks at length to an audience of real or imagined people, or to himself, employs the device of monologue. With respect to narrative, however, monologue appears in the two devices known as soliloquy and internal monologue.

Soliloquy is the presentation in actual speech of the thoughts of a character while the speaker is alone. Soliloquy might be described as external monologue. Hamlet's famous soliloquy "To be, or not to be" is a good example.

Internal monologue is a dramatic presentation of the thoughts of a character phrased in the language of speech but not given vocal utterance. This device may or may not be set off with quotation marks. In the following examples the first is so distinguished and the second is not.

"The devil," he thought. "People awake! some student or some saint, confound the crew! Can't they get drunk and lie in bed snoring like their neighbors! What's the good of curfew, and poor devils of bell-ringers jumping at a rope's end in bell-towers? What's the use of day, if people sit up all night? The gripes to them." He grinned as he saw where his logic was leading him.[1]

He drew back and rose to his feet with a revulsion of fear, then grew calm.

This is not she, not Slim Girl, Brave Alone, not Came With War, not my wife. This is something she left behind. It is dead, it never had life; it was she inside it who gave it life. I am not afraid of it, and can I ever be afraid of you, oh, beautiful? I shall be calm, I shall bury it, a Navajo burial.

He knelt beside her body and began to sob.[2]

Indirect discourse is the narrative method of representing the speeches and thoughts of characters by indirect, or non-dramatic means. In indirect discourse the speech or thought is not directly expressed by the character but is reported by the writer in the form of a summary or paraphrase. Usually, therefore, the past tense is used in place of the present tense employed in direct discourse.

Indirect discourse may be used alone or in combination with the various methods of direct discourse. In the two examples following it stands alone: in the first, as a summary of speech; and in the second, as a paraphrase of thought.

When Mr. Brownlow admitted that on no one point of inquiry could he yet return a satisfactory answer; and that he had postponed any investigation into Oliver's previous his-

[1] From Robert Louis Stevenson, *A Lodging for the Night.* By permission of Charles Scribner's Sons.

[2] From Oliver La Farge, *Laughing Boy.* By permission of Houghton Mifflin Company.

tory until he thought the boy was strong enough to bear it; Mr. Grimwig chuckled maliciously. And he demanded, with a sneer, whether the housekeeper was in the habit of counting the plate at night; because, if she didn't find a tablespoon or two missing some sunshiny morning, why, he would be content to—and so forth.

(Dickens, *Oliver Twist*)

This afternoon, the sight of Bob's cheerful freckled face had given her discontent a new direction. She thought it was part of the hardship of her life that there was laid upon her the burthen of larger wants than others seemed to feel—that she had to endure this wide hopeless yearning for that something, whatever it was, that was greatest and best on this earth. She wished she could have been like Bob, with his easily satisfied ignorance, or like Tom, who had something to do on which he could fix his mind with a steady purpose, and disregard everything else.

(George Eliot, *The Mill on the Floss*)

The following is an example of indirect discourse combined with two bits of direct discourse, one of speech and one of thought.

He began to speak as soon as he saw me. I had been very long on the road. He could not wait. Had to start without me. The up-river stations had to be relieved. There had been so many delays already that he did not know who was dead and who was alive, and how they got on—and so on, and so on. He paid no attention to my explanations, and, playing with a stick of sealing-wax, repeated several times that the situation was "very grave, very grave." There were rumors that a very important station was in jeopardy, and its chief, Mr. Kurtz, was ill. Hoped it was not true. Mr. Kurtz was . . . I felt weary and irritable. Hang Kurtz, I thought.[3]

[3] From *Heart of Darkness,* by Joseph Conrad, copyright, 1903, 1925, by Doubleday, Doran & Company, Inc.

EXPOSITION

Exposition is the method employed in explaining the nature of things, machines, people, situations, conditions and ideas. It is the imparting of knowledge by setting forth, clearly and definitively, the elements of its subject and explaining their organic and functional interrelationships. Its purpose is to secure complete understanding of its subject. Although this understanding may be aided and emphasized by such simple devices as comparisons and contrasts, and by the listing of examples and illustrations, it depends primarily upon two methods of explanation: definition and analysis, alone or in combination.

Definition, or classification, is the method of revealing the nature of a subject by restricting it in terms of (1) its genus, or the class to which it belongs, and (2) its differentiæ, or the qualities which distinguish it from other members of its class. In other words, the writer discovers and states the class or group to which the object of his definition belongs, and then he tries to discover and state the qualities, attributes, or distinguishing characteristics which make his subject different from other members of the same class.

This process may be illustrated by briefly defining a watch. The class to which a watch belongs is that which includes all time keepers, or instruments for keeping and indicating time. But this class includes a number of such instruments: the mechanical clock, the water clock, the horologe, the sundial, the hourglass, and so forth. In order to define the watch, therefore, we must observe how it differs from other instruments in its class.

After a brief examination of a watch we discover that it differs from the horologe, sundial, and hourglass in that it is *mechanical,* that is, its actuating force is a system of springs and gears. But the mechanical clock is also so actuated. Obviously, however, the watch differs from the mechanical clock in size, since it is designed to fit a pocket. (The wrist watch, of course, is simply another kind of watch.) We arrive therefore at this definition: a watch is an instrument for keeping and indicating time (genus), actuated by a system of springs and gears, and made small enough to fit a pocket (differentiæ).

Analysis, or exposition by division, is a process exactly opposite to that of definition. In analysis the whole is considered, not in terms of other wholes, but in terms of its own component parts and internal organization. The subject is dissected, and each part is explained separately and in its relations to the whole or to other parts.

This process may be illustrated by indicating briefly how one might proceed to analyze a watch. Upon examination it will be found that a watch consists of a *case* which encloses the *works,* a *back* which can be removed, a *face* equipped with *hands* and protected by a *crystal,* a *stem* with a *ratchet* for winding, a *ring* to which a chain or fob may be attached, and, internally, a complicated system of *springs, gears, pinions, jewels,* etc., which we shall not attempt to analyze further. The complete analysis of the watch would include a listing and naming of each internal part with a full explanation of its relationship to other parts and to the watch as a whole.

ARGUMENTATION

Argumentation is the method of presenting a subject in such a way as to secure, not merely comprehension of it, but also a conviction that the provided interpretation of it is correct. It attempts to demonstrate the logical relationships between various facts, between various ideas, or between facts and ideas. The conclusion of its demonstration is the proof of a thesis or proposition. Although argument employs many devices appealing to the intellect (see p. 53), its chief methods of presentation are two: deductive reasoning and inductive reasoning.

Deductive reasoning is the method of demonstrating relationships between accepted generalizations, or known truths, and unaccepted statements, or propositions. The regular, precise form of this method of reasoning is called the syllogism. A syllogism consists of three statements. The first, which is known as the major premise, is the statement of a generally accepted truth. The second, known as the minor premise, is the statement of a specific fact. The minor premise is related to the major premise by a term which is common to both. On the logical principle that things equal to the same thing are equal to each other, therefore, a third statement, or conclusion, may be deduced by cancelling the common term and equating what remains. Following is the classic example of the syllogism:

Major premise: All men are mortal.

Minor premise: Socrates is a man.

Conclusion: Therefore Socrates is mortal.

Inductive reasoning, on the other hand, is the method of arriving at the statement of a new general truth by assuming that, because the statement is true in every known case, it is therefore true in all possible cases. It is thus evident that the method of inductive reasoning depends for its success upon two factors: the scrupulous accumulation of all available evidence and the assumption that the available evidence is sufficiently comprehensive to be conclusive. The weakness of the method is the unknown factor of the unavailable evidence. Thus one may observe that a swan is white. The further observation of a large number of swans may establish the fact that each swan observed is white. One may then arrive at the generalization that all swans are white. And the generalization holds true until someone happens to observe a swan of another color. Nevertheless, despite this possibility of error, it is the generalizations arrived at by inductive reasoning and supported by wide experience that inevitably serve as the major premises of all deductive reasoning.

II. Mechanics of Appeal

The mechanics of prompting a co-operative response in the reader depend largely upon two important properties of words. Words, taken singly or in combination, not only state specifically what they mean, but also mean as much as they imply. To these two properties of words are given the names, denotation and connotation. The **denotation** of a word is the meaning of that word as determined by the specific object, idea, or process of which it stands as the name. The **connotation** of a word is the whole fringe of emotions, memories, and suggested ideas which association has come to attach to the word. Thus there is an important shade of difference in the final meaning of such words, often etymologically equivalent, as "domestic" and "homely," "lovely" and "erotic," "servant" and "serf," "brassy" and "brazen."

In appealing to his reader the literary artist has at his disposal all the denotative and connotative resources of language. Specifically, he may provide a direct or indirect stimulus to the senses; he may attempt to start a train of associations; or he may quicken a response of intellectual activity. A detailed discussion of the mechanics of these various appeals follows.

A. Appeal to the Senses

Literature makes its appeal to the senses by endeavoring to stimulate a response in the reader's senses of sight, touch, taste, smell, and hearing. But the medium of literature is words. Now it is perfectly obvious that the only quality of a word which can give a direct stimulus to the senses is its sound. The sound of a word, when spoken, falls upon the ear and directly stimulates the sense of hearing. Indeed, relatively speaking, one may say that the sound value of a word exists irrespective of its meaning. The sound value of words can be appreciated even when they happen to be in a language which one does not understand.

The stimulus imparted by a word to the other four senses, however, is not a direct, but an indirect, stimulus. That is to say, the sensuous value of a word, apart from sound, depends upon its meaning. In order that one may have the sensation of sight, touch, taste, or smell, it is necessary that one be conscious of the concrete stimulus which produces the sensation. Of this stimulus the word stands as the name. For instance, a painter may apply to canvas the color *green* and produce immediately in an observer a definite sensuous reaction. But before the word "green" can produce a similar sensuous experience, it is necessary for a reader to understand the meaning of the word and to associate with the word the thing for which it stands. Thus words which attempt to stimulate the senses of sight, touch, taste, and smell, do so by prompting a sensuous response to the mental image created by their meaning.

For this reason, literature really makes its appeal to the senses in two ways. First, it endeavors to stimulate the senses of sight, touch, taste, and smell by creating in the mind of the reader a vivid and immediate awareness of an object or other stimulus which will quicken those senses. And, second, it tries to prompt in the reader a primary reaction to sound. The first of these practices is known as imagery. The second has to do with rhythm and tone color. A detailed discussion of both follows.

IMAGERY

Imagery is the process of making thought vivid by presenting it to the mind in the form of pictures or images which will stimulate the senses. Its primary appeal is sensuous, not rational. It translates the abstract into the concrete, the general or indefinite into the specific and precise. Although its most natural appeal is to the sense of sight, at times it also attempts to stimulate the senses of touch, taste, and smell. Only the sense of hearing is excluded from its province.

[The term *imagery* is also used collectively to designate the product of the image-making process.]

Admirable illustrations of imagery and of its appeals to the various senses may be drawn from the work of the most sensuous of English poets, John Keats. For vivid painting of pictures consider the following:

> A chain-drooped lamp was flickering by each door;
> The arras, rich with horseman, hawk, and hound,
> Fluttered in the besieging wind's uproar;
> And the long carpets rose along the gusty floor.
> > (*The Eve of St. Agnes*)

As an appeal to the sense of smell:

> I cannot see what flowers are at my feet,
>   Nor what soft incense hangs upon the boughs,
> But, in embalmèd darkness, guess each sweet
>   Wherewith the seasonable month endows
> The grass, the thicket, and the fruit-tree wild.
> > (*Ode to a Nightingale*)

As an appeal to taste:

> Aye, in the very temple of Delight
>   Veiled Melancholy has her sovran shrine,

Though seen of none save him whose strenuous tongue
Can burst Joy's grape against his palate fine.

(Ode on Melancholy)

A remarkable appeal to the sense of touch and feeling in general is the following:

St. Agnes' Eve—ah, bitter chill it was!
The owl, for all his feathers, was a-cold;
The hare limped trembling through the frozen grass,
And silent was the flock in woolly fold.
Numb were the Beadsman's fingers, while he told
His rosary, and while his frosted breath,
Like pious incense from a censer old,
Seemed taking flight for heaven, without a death,
Past the sweet Virgin's picture, while his prayer he saith.

(The Eve of St. Agnes)

Although, in the main, imagery is used to gain vividness by means of concreteness and precision, it may sometimes reverse the process. Thus certain very impressive effects may be gained by presenting the apparently familiar and definite in terms of vagueness and indefiniteness. The following example is Milton's famous imaginative realization of Death:

The other Shape—
If shape it might be called that shape had none
Distinguishable in member, joint, or limb;
Or substance might be called that shadow seemed,
For each seemed either—black it stood as Night,
Fierce as ten Furies, terrible as Hell,
And shook a dreadful dart: what seemed his head
The likeness of a kingly crown had on.

(Paradise Lost, Bk. II)

Through the use of imagery the literary artist expresses his thoughts figuratively. This figurative expression often resolves itself into certain recognizable rhetorical devices known as **figures of speech.** The most important of these, in so far as they pertain to imagery, are described below.

The **symbol** is perhaps the most important of all figures of speech, especially in poetry. Indeed, a poem itself may be considered a literary symbol of an experience. A symbol is anything used to represent some other object or idea which it resembles. As such a representative, its significance is determined not by its own proper meaning but by the meaning of that for which it stands. The purpose of the substitution is usually to gain clarity, simplicity, and concreteness. **Symbolism** is that kind of thought or expression which is characterized by the use of symbols. Examples of symbols may be found in the albatross which figures in Coleridge's *Rime of the Ancient Mariner,* in the scarlet A of Hawthorne's *The Scarlet Letter,* in the raven of Poe's poem of that name. Wordsworth symbolizes the sense of a conscious life force, which he finds lacking in modern appreciation of nature, in the mythological figures of the following:

>   Great God! I'd rather be
> A pagan suckled in a creed outworn;
> So might I, standing on this pleasant lea,
> Have glimpses that would make me less forlorn;
> Have sight of Proteus rising from the sea;
> Or hear old Triton blow his wreathèd horn.
>   (*The World is Too Much with Us*)

The most common sort of imagery is that designed to render colorful, distinctive, and immediate what might otherwise appear colorless and vague. Of this sort are the figures known as epithet, personification, apostrophe, and vision.

Epithet is a qualifying term applied to a person or thing for the purpose of giving it vividness and distinctive individuality, as in the following:

> Oft of one wide expanse had I been told
> That *deep-browed* Homer ruled as his demesne.
> (Keats, *On First Looking into Chapman's Homer*)

> The breezy call of *incense-breathing* morn.
> (Gray, *Elegy*)

In certain kinds of poetry such epithets frequently become conventionalized and appear regularly in the descriptive qualifiers of certain common words. From the origins of the use, these are known as **epic epithets.** Such are Homer's "*crafty* Odysseus" and Virgil's "*pious* Æneas," as well as other epic expressions like "*wine-dark* sea," "*rosy-fingered* dawn," and "*far-darting* Apollo."

The **kenning** appears in old Germanic poetry as a somewhat extended and altered form of the epithet. A kenning is a conventionalized descriptive word or expression used as the substitute for a more common and familiar word. For the word "sea," for instance, occur such kennings as "the whale-road," "the bath of the seagull"; for "ship," "the foamy-necked floater," etc.

Personification is the treatment of an inanimate object or of an abstract quality as though it were a living person. The value of personification is that it endows the abstract and lifeless with qualities natural and immediately applicable to human beings, as in

> Haste thee, nymph, and bring with thee
> Jest, and youthful Jollity, . . .
> Sport that wrinkled Care derides,
> And Laughter holding both his sides.
> (Milton, *L'Allegro*)

Apostrophe is an abrupt change from ordinary discourse to direct address in the second person. Occurring frequently with personification, it usually takes the form of eulogy or supplication. Its value lies in the sense of immediacy imparted by its exclamatory and dramatic quality. For example:

> Milton! thou shouldst be living at this hour:
> England hath need of thee . . .
> (Wordsworth, *London, 1802*)

> O Rome! my Country! City of the Soul!
> The orphans of the heart must turn to thee.
> (Byron, *Childe Harold's Pilgrimage*)

Vision is the picturing of something remote in space or time as though it were present before the writer, and hence the reader. A good example is found in the poet Byron's meditation upon the ruined Coliseum:

> I see before me the Gladiator lie:
> He leans upon his hand—his manly brow
> Consents to death, but conquers agony,
> And his droop'd head sinks gradually low—
> And through his side the last drops, ebbing slow
> From the red gash, fall heavy, one by one,

Like the first of a thunder-shower; and now
The arena swims around him—he is gone,
Ere ceased the inhuman shout which hail'd the
    wretch who won.

(Childe Harold's Pilgrimage)

Another kind of imagery is that which strives for clarity and vividness through the illustration of its subject by comparison with something which it resembles. The common types of this sort of imagery are simile and metaphor.

Simile (a name derived from the Latin adjective meaning "like") is a form of comparison which specifically states that one thing is *like* another.

O, my luve is like a red, red rose,
    That's newly sprung in June:
O, my luve is like a melodie
    That's sweetly played in tune.
        (Burns, *A Red, Red Rose*)

Life, like a dome of many-coloured glass,
Stains the white radiance of Eternity,
Until Death tramples it to fragments.
        (Shelly, *Adonais*)

Epic simile is a variety of simile in which one member of the comparison is expanded for purposes of detailed illustration. As its name implies, it is one of the chief devices for imaginative embellishment used in epic poetry. Thus Milton describes the assembling of Satan's host in the hall of Pandemonium:

As bees
In spring-time, when the Sun with Taurus rides,
Pour forth their populous youth about the hive

In clusters; they among fresh dews and flowers
Fly to and fro, or on the smoothed plank,
The suburb of their straw-built citadel,
New rubbed with balm, expatiate, and confer
Their state affairs: so thick the aëry crowd
Swarmed and were straightened.
(Paradise Lost, Bk. I)

Metaphor is an implied rather than a specifically stated simile. It is more striking and emphatic than simile in that it states, not that one thing is *like* another, but that it *is* another, which it resembles. Its value lies in the emphasis given to those qualities which form the basis of similarity between the two things compared.

Yet all experience is an arch wherethrough
Gleams that untravelled world, whose margin fades
Forever and forever when I move.
(Tennyson, Ulysses)

In most uses of metaphorical language the comparison is merely implied as in the beginning of Swinburne's Chorus:

When the hounds of spring are on winter's traces,
The mother of months in meadow or plain
Fills the shadows and windy places
With lisp of leaves and ripple of rain.[4]

Conceit is a specialized, and somewhat far-fetched, form of the comparison implicit in simile and metaphor, which flourished in English literature during the sixteenth

[4] From Algernon Charles Swinburne, *Atalanta in Calydon.* By permission of Harper & Brothers.

and seventeenth centuries. It is a fine-drawn and audacious association of two objects or conceptions which depends for its value not so much upon the essential truth of the comparison as upon the ingenuity displayed in detecting any similarity at all. The following illustrate two varieties of conceit.

> There is a garden in her face,
> Where roses and white lilies grow;
> A heav'nly paradise is that place,
> Wherein all pleasant fruits do flow.
> There cherries grow which none may buy
> Till cherry-ripe themselves do cry.
> (Campion, *There is a Garden*)

> Our two souls therefore, which are one,
> Though I must go, endure not yet
> A breach, but an expansion,
> Like gold to airy thinness beat.
> (Donne, *Valediction Forbidding
> Mourning*)

Besides those referred to above there are several rhetorical figures which are also an important part of literary style. In some of them imagery is an important element; in others it plays a subordinate part. These figures are synecdoche, metonymy, hyperbole, and litotes.

Synecdoche is the use of a word which indicates a part in place of one which indicates a whole, or the reverse. The following illustrate both forms.

> There the river eddy whirls,
> And there the surly village churls,

> And the *red cloaks* of market girls,
>   Pass onward from Shalott.
>   (Tennyson, *The Lady of Shalott*)

> . . . oft in whirls the mad tornado flies,
> Mingling the *ravaged landscape* with the skies.
>   (Goldsmith, *The Deserted Village*)

Metonymy is the substitution, for the name of a thing, of a word which designates one of its attributes and thus suggests the thing. The purpose is thus to emphasize that particular attribute which for the moment is most significant.

> What idle progeny succeed
> To chase the *rolling circle's speed*
> Or urge the flying ball?
>   (Gray, *Ode on a Distant
>   Prospect of Eton College*)

> Along the lawn, where scatter'd hamlets rose,
> *Unwieldy wealth* and *cumbrous pomp* repose.
>   (Goldsmith, *The Deserted Village*)

Hyperbole is obvious and deliberate exaggeration for the purpose of emphasizing the strong emotion behind an assertion. A famous instance of hyperbole is the speech of Faustus to the phantom of Helen of Troy in Marlowe's play, *Dr. Faustus:*

> Was this the face that launched a thousand ships?
> And burnt the topless towers of Ilium? . . .
> O thou art fairer than the evening air
> Clad in the beauty of a thousand stars,
> Brighter art thou than flaming Jupiter
> When he appeared to hapless Semele,
> More lovely than the monarch of the sky

> In wanton Arethusa's azured arms,
> And none but thou shalt be my paramour.

Litotes is the opposite of hyperbole. It is obvious and deliberate understatement, frequently employing a negative to emphasize the opposite affirmative.

> Oh, sir, she smiled, no doubt,
> Whene'er I passed her; but who passed without
> Much the same smile? This grew; I gave commands;
> *Then all smiles stopped together.*
> (Browning, *My Last Duchess*)

The value of litotes for humorous effect may be illustrated by John Gilpin's rueful remark in the midst of his wild ride:

> "Stop, stop, John Gilpin!—Here's the house,"
>   They all at once did cry;
> "The dinner waits, and we are tired."
>   Said Gilpin—"So am I."
>   (Cowper, *The Diverting History
>   of John Gilpin*)

Closely related to figures of speech are several mechanical devices frequently used for their imaginative appeal. These, it must be understood, are *not* figures of speech, but extensions of the basic principles of certain figures of speech, notably metaphor. For metaphor is the root of figurative expression: namely, the substitution of a simple graphic symbol for something less familiar and clear. But metaphorical expression may be simple and restricted or it may be expanded and complex. In the latter form it may comprise a whole unit of a larger composition, or, indeed, an independent composition in itself. Of such character are the mechanical devices known as allegory, fable or apologue, and parable.

Allegory is a greatly expanded and detailed metaphor used to expound, largely by means of personification and symbolism, a complex abstraction in terms of story, action, and human nature. The most famous allegories of English literature are Bunyan's *Pilgrim's Progress,* Spenser's *The Faerie Queene,* and the anonymous play *Everyman.*

Fable and **apologue** are brief fictitious narratives so designed that from them may be deduced an obvious moral lesson. Apologue is the more general term. Fable differs from apologue in that the story is usually concerned with the activities of animals endowed with human attributes. The most familiar fables are those of the Greek Æsop. Dickens's *Christmas Carol* is a familiar apologue.

[The word *fable* is also used, in a different sense, to denote the *story* or *plot* of a poem or drama.]

Parable is to the fable or apologue what simile is to metaphor. It is brief fictitious narrative with a moral, used to illustrate concretely the meaning of an abstract idea. As in the case of the simile, it is frequently introduced by the word *like* or some equivalent expression. The best-known parables are those of Jesus as recounted in the New Testament.

RHYTHM

The second of the sensuous appeals of literature is that of sound. Of the sound values of literature there are two familiar varieties, known as tone-color and rhythm. The former of these is more appropriately considered in connection with poetry (see p. 157). The latter is treated below.

Rhythm is the ebb and flow, or lilt, imparted to speech, through modulation of the voice, by the variation in emphasis devoted to spoken words or syllables. All speech is to a certain extent rhythmic, but speech rhythms may vary widely in character. It is a phenomenon of speech that strong emotion tends to produce in it a more pronounced rhythm.

Rhythm depends for its effects upon a natural property of language, namely accent or stress. All polysyllabic words bear a normal accent upon one syllable. [*morning, before, plentiful.*] Phrases likewise have a normal accent. [*in the morning, before noon, from the memory.*] When words and phrases, however, are grouped in larger units of expression, the value of their normal accent may vary widely in relation to the emphasis of the passage as a whole. In the words and phrases given above, when considered separately, there is little difference in the stress given to accented syllables. When combined in the following sentence, however, observe how the accented syllables vary in relative emphasis:

Early in the morning the dew is plentiful, but long before noon it has vanished even from memory.

Obviously the sense demands that the syllables *Ear, plen, long,* and *mem* receive greater emphasis than *morn, noon,* and *van,* even though the latter are stressed more than other normally accented syllables. It is this variation of stress, coupled with the tonal quality of the syllables, which provides the phenomenon of rhythm.

Rhythm is common to both poetry and prose. It may be either regular or irregular. Rhythm which is arranged according to a regular and uniform pattern is spoken of as verse. Prose rhythm is marked by irregularity and a studious avoidance of uniformity. But whether rhythm is arranged according to a regular or an irregular pattern, it is capable of achieving amazingly subtle and pleasurable effects. These may serve as a reënforcement to the sense of the passage, as the means of evoking a mood appropriate to the occasion, or, irrespective of meaning, merely as an æsthetic delight to the ear.

The mechanics of rhythm admit of the most elaborate analysis and codification, into which it is unnecessary to enter except for detailed study of rhetorical science. Their application, however, is one of the most important elements of artistic literary style. In this general application the matter of sentence rhythm is of major consequence.

Since rhythm depends upon words and syllables in combination, the basic unit of rhythm is the sentence. Sentences, of course, have a fundamental logical structure; but in addition they usually possess a corresponding rhythmical pattern. This **sentence rhythm** is of four principal varieties illustrated in four corresponding types of sentence: the simple sentence, the loose sentence, the periodic sentence, and the balanced sentence.

The **simple sentence,** as its name implies, is the simplest complete unit of expression. Devoted to the expression of one complete thought, it is brief, direct, and lucid. Within the single sentence the rhythm is of necessity simple and rudimentary, although variable according to the quantity and kind of modifying elements included. But in a series, simple sentences are capable of the most varied rhythmic modulation, from a placid, easy succession like swells upon the sea to the sharp, staccato speed of a machine gun.

No answer still. I thrust a torch through the remaining aperture and let it fall within. There came forth in return only a jingling of the bells. My heart grew sick—on account of the dampness of the catacombs. I hastened to make an end of my labor. I forced the last stone into its position; I plastered it up. Against the new masonry I re-erected the old rampart of bones. For the half of a century no mortal has disturbed them. *In pace requiescat!*

(Poe, *The Cask of Amontillado*)

The **loose** or **cumulative sentence** is of supreme value in cultivating subtle modulations of rhythm. From the standpoint of logical structure, the loose sentence is a complex accumulation of various independent and dependent clauses and phrases, which moves to a conclusion by a meandering process of accretion without obvious climactic effect. It is here referred to as cumulative because of the incremental method whereby are achieved its characteristic rhythmic effects. Because of its varied and rambling texture it is the most flexible of sentences and admits of the widest range of harmonic modulations.

It is a favorite sentence form among conscious rhythmic stylists.

Every glade of grass burned like the golden floor of heaven, opening in sudden gleams as the foliage broke and closed above it, as sheet-lightning opens in a cloud at sunset; the motionless masses of dark rock—dark though flushed with scarlet lichen, casting their quiet shadows across its restless radiance, the fountain underneath them filling its marble hollow with blue mist and fitful sound; and over all, the multitudinous bars of amber and rose, the sacred clouds that have no darkness, and only exist to illumine, were seen in fathomless intervals between the solemn and arbed repose of the stone pines, passing to lose themselves in the last, white, blinding lustre of the measureless line where the Campagna melted into the blaze of the sea.

(Ruskin, *Modern Painters*)

The **periodic sentence** is as complex as the loose sentence but much more formal in structure. It is so constructed that a series of dependent elements, incomplete in themselves, are held in suspension until the concluding statement of the sentence brings them to a focus and completes the sense. Rhythmically it is of value for its climactic effect of crescendo and suspense, like that of a wave rolling up until its crest can be sustained no longer and it breaks upon the shore.

Since, therefore, the knowledge and survey of vice is in this world so necessary to the constituting of human virtue, and the scanning of error to the confirmation of truth, how can we more safely, and with less danger, scout into the regions of sin and falsity, than by reading all manner of tractates and hearing all manner of reason?

(Milton, *Areopagitica*)

The **balanced sentence** is quite as formal as the periodic but is based upon a different principle. It is a sentence composed of corresponding elements parallel in structure. Its effect is one of alternation, of echo. Rhythmically its movement is that of the pendulum rather than that of the breaking wave or the winding stream. Frequently antithetical in structure, its rhythm is correspondingly antiphonal.

You could not be put in prison for speaking against industry, but you can be sent to Coventry for speaking like a fool.[5]

For friendship maketh indeed a fair day in the affections, from storm and tempest; but it maketh daylight in the understanding, out of darkness and confusion of thoughts.
(Bacon, *Of Friendship*)

From the foregoing it may be seen that a practically limitless rhythmic modulation may be achieved by judicious arrangement of sentence elements and by the use of the various kinds of sentences. Nevertheless, whatever the kind or organization, certain parts of the sentence are of major importance for rhythm: namely, the concluding syllables of major clauses and of the sentence as a whole. Here, if anywhere, the rhythmic effect must be one of ease, appropriateness, finality, and beauty. Such a concluding rhythm is known as a **cadence** (from the Latin word meaning a "falling"), and marks the fall of the voice from sound to silence. Note the varied rhythmic

[5] From Robert Louis Stevenson, *An Apology for Idlers*. By permission of Charles Scribner's Sons.

patterns of the italicized cadences in the following passage:

The number of the dead long *exceédeth all that shall live*. The night of time *far surpasseth the day*, and who knows *when was the Æquinox?* Every hour adds unto that *current arithmetic*, which scarce *stands one moment*. And since death must be the *Lucina of life*, and even Pagans could doubt whether *thus to live, were to die;* since our longest sun sets at *right descensions*, and makes but *winter arches*, and therefore, it cannot be long before we lie *down in darkness*, and have our *light in ashes;* since the brother of death daily haunts us *with dying mementos*, and time that grows old itself bids us *hope no long duration: diuturnity is a dream* and *folly of expectation*.

(Sir Thomas Browne, Urn Burial)

B. APPEAL TO ASSOCIATION

Words, besides having the power of calling up images and of creating sound effects, also have the power of stimulating associations. This associative property of words affords a second aid to the writer in suggesting indirectly the richness of his meaning and in enlisting the co-operative response of his reader.

The method of association, however, differs from that of imagery. Imagery depends for its effectiveness upon a process of calling up before the mind's eye images as immediately present and thus directly stimulative to the senses. Association, on the other hand, draws upon the past, upon the conscious or unconscious memory. It re-enforces the specific meaning of a word or phrase with additional shades of meaning and feeling attached to it in the reader's mind through past experience. The peculiar advantage of association is that it supplements the artist's powers of description and suggestion with a positive contribution on the part of the reader from his own individual experience.

Associations, it may thus be seen, are both emotional (and therefore fundamentally sensuous) and intellectual. Some words are more powerful than others because of the deeper feeling they produce, and accordingly may vary in value from one reader to another. Such words, for instance, as "God," "mother," and "home" have such obvious emotional value that tawdry over-use has cast upon them the suspicion of cheap sentimentality. Other words depend for their value upon breadth and richness of knowledge, upon wide acquaintance with historical, traditional, and literary associations. Thus to the informed there is a world of difference between the implications of "China" and "Cathay," of "the streets of Ispahan" and "the sidewalks of New York." Obviously in this latter case the value of association depends entirely upon the background of the reader, just as in the former it depends upon the reader's emotional responsiveness. In the following example consider the associative value of the italicized words:

> Thou wast not born for death, immortal Bird!
> No *hungry generations* tread thee down;
> The voice I hear this passing night was heard
> In *ancient days* by *emperor* and *clown:*

> Perhaps the self-same song that found a path
> Through the *sad heart of Ruth,* when, *sick for home,*
> She stood in tears *amid the alien corn;*
> The same that oft-times hath
> Charm'd *magic casements,* opening on the foam
> Of *perilous seas,* in *faëry lands forlorn.*
>   (Keats, *Ode to a Nightingale*)

The principle of association has, of course, the widest and most varied application in literature. Indeed the application is universal and well-nigh inevitable. As a conscious device, however, it has particular value as a means of evoking a recognition of specialized and distinctive groups, minds, and temperaments, localized types of life and character, and the characteristics of historical periods. Especially useful is this kind of association for writers of "local color" stories and historical romances. It is this application of the associative principle which dictated Spenser's deliberate archaism in *The Faerie Queene;* by means of which Thackeray, through the careful use of "period language," endeavored to recreate the spirit of the eighteenth century in *Henry Esmond;* and which gives their peculiar flavor to Joel Chandler Harris's Uncle Remus stories, Twain's *Huckleberry Finn,* and Stevenson's *Treasure Island.* As a specific example, consider the value in *Treasure Island* of the pirate chanty ending "yo, ho, ho, and a bottle of rum!"

An important extension of the associative principle is found in allusion. **Allusion** is a method of enlarging the significance of a statement or situation by referring it to something familiar in the reader's memory. Thus when

Byron speaks of Rome as "the Niobe of nations," he not only strikes off a brilliant metaphor but enriches his meaning with the utmost economy of means.

Allusion is commonly found in two slightly different forms. There is first what may be called **historical allusion.** This is an allusion to some fact or event of the historical, legendary, or literary past, the general circumstances and meaning of which are related to the immediate subject through the use of a key word or phrase which recalls them to the memory. Such are the following:

> Now in the sea's red vintage melts the sun,
>   As Egypt's pearl dissolved in rosy wine,
> And Cleopatra night drinks all. 'Tis done,
>   Love, lay thine hand in mine.
> (Lanier, Evening Song) [6]

> The isles of Greece, the isles of Greece!
>   Where burning Sappho loved and sung,
> Where grew the arts of war and peace,—
>   Where Delos rose and Phœbus sprung!
> Eternal summer gilds them yet,
> But all, except their sun, is set.
> (Byron, Don Juan)

A second form of allusion may be called the **literary allusion.** Of a more subtle order than the other, this form proceeds by means of partial quotation or paraphrase to suggest a familiar passage from some other work of literature, a recognition of which in connection with its general context serves to give additional significance to

[6] By permission of Charles Scribner's Sons.

the passage wherein the allusion occurs. In the following excerpt Lowell makes effective use of a familiar passage in *The Merchant of Venice:*

> After a few such experiences, I, for one, have felt as if I were merely one of those horrid things preserved in spirits (and very bad spirits, too) in a cabinet. I was not the fellow-being of these explorers: I was a curiosity; I was a specimen. *Hath not* an American *organs, dimensions, senses, affections, passions even as* a European hath? *If you prick us, do we not bleed? If you tickle us, do we not laugh?* I will not keep on with Shylock to his next question but one.
>
> (*On a Certain Condescension in Foreigners*)

As with association in general, the value of allusion depends upon the knowledge and cultural background of the reader. Obviously certain cultural standards must be met before a reader is prepared for allusive literature. For the same reason much poetry is difficult and obscure in direct proportion to the reader's general ignorance. For the reasonably educated reader, however, association and allusion have certain distinct advantages. Apart from their value as pure embellishment: (1) They provide a wealth of illustration, explanation, and reënforcement of their subject while maintaining an economic brevity and conciseness. (2) They give added significance to the immediate subject by relating the present to the cherished past of human thought and experience. (3) They enlist the positive co-operation of the reader in interpreting the full meaning of the artist's experience.

C. Appeal to the Intellect

In addition to stimulating the senses and appealing to the associative faculties, the literary artist endeavors to enlist the co-operative interest of the reader by producing purely intellectual reactions. That is, the writer attempts to illuminate his subject by inducing in the reader an intellectual activity which is usually critical and judicial. The fundamental process is one of comparison and contrast. This may be either explicit or implicit. That is, the comparison or contrast may be specifically stated, in which case the reader is called upon merely to weigh and approve the justice and appropriateness of the comparison; or it may be implied, in which case the reader must complete the comparison or contrast from his own knowledge through the keenness of his perception, and confirm its pertinence by his critical judgment.

As in the case of sensuous appeal, the general principles which underlie the appeal to the intellect are most simply exemplified in several figures of speech. The nature of these, however, is not sensuous but intellectual. These figures of speech are known as analogy, antithesis, and irony.

Analogy is a form of comparison which extends the principle of simile by calling attention to the resemblance of certain complex relationships, functions, and processes. In poetry analogy and epic simile often mean practically the same thing. The following is a famous analogy:

Many were the wit-combats betwixt him (Shakespeare) and Ben Jonson; which two I behold like a Spanish great galleon and an English man-of-war: Master Jonson (like the former) was built far higher in learning; solid, but slow, in his performances. Shakespeare, with the English man-of-war, lesser in bulk, but lighter in sailing, could turn with all tides, tack about, and take advantage of all winds, by the quickness of his wit and invention.

(Fuller, *Worthies of England*)

Antithesis is the careful balance of one object, statement, condition, or idea against another for the purpose of contrast. Frequently antithesis is extended to the phraseology in which the balance is expressed, as in the following:

Foxes have holes, and birds of the air have nests; but the Son of man hath not where to lay his head.

(*Gospel according to St. Luke* x, 58)

A more elaborate example of antithesis is contained in the latter part of the illustration quoted under analogy.

Irony is implied contrast. Its usual form is a statement of the opposite of what is meant, but made in such a manner that the true meaning remains obvious. An excellent example of sustained irony is the familiar funeral oration of Antony over the body of Cæsar in Shakespeare's *Julius Cæsar*. As a single instance:

Will you be patient? Will you stay awhile?
I have o'ershot myself to tell you of it.
I fear I wrong the honourable men
Whose daggers have stabb'd Cæsar; I do fear it.

[The method of irony when employed for the purpose of a taunt or jeer is known as **sarcasm.** For example, the tart reply of Job to the smug Zophar, who has just completed a definitive exposition of ultimate truth: "No doubt but ye are the people, and wisdom shall die with you." (*Job* xii, 2)]

Besides the simple figures of speech referred to above, the mechanics of intellectual appeal include a number of more elaborate devices, which vary widely in the degree of their complexity. Once again be it noted that these are *not* figures of speech, but extensions of the principles upon which the figures of speech given above are based. That is, the following devices involve a process of comparison or contrast, and depend for their effect upon the intellectual keenness and critical judgment of the reader.

In these devices certain characteristic and common features may be observed. (1) They utilize comparison and contrast for the purpose of stressing incongruity, especially that sort of incongruity which represents a discrepancy between the subject under consideration and some abstract standard of value set up either explicitly or implicitly in the mind of both writer and reader. (2) The object of the device is the prompting of a critical response. This critical response is usually a rejection or repudiation of that which is represented as incongruous with the accepted standard. (3) To a greater or less degree this critical rejection is accomplished through, and indicated by, laughter.

Of these devices the two basic and most simple are humor and wit. **Humor** is a device for producing laughter or amusement by simply calling attention to the obvious and universally recognizable incongruities of life, and by emphasizing their inherent absurdity. In the main, the mood of humor is tolerant, genial, and pleasant.

The following is a good example of Washington Irving's characteristic humor:

A fine lady, in those times, waddled under more clothes, even on a fair summer's day, than would have clad the whole bevy of a modern ball-room. Nor were they the less admired by the gentlemen in consequence thereof. On the contrary, the greatness of a lover's passion seemed to increase in proportion to the magnitude of its object,—and a voluminous damsel, arrayed in a dozen of petticoats, was declared by a Low-Dutch sonneteer of the province to be radiant as a sunflower, and luxuriant as a full-blown cabbage. Certain it is, that in those days the heart of a lover could not contain more than one lady at a time; whereas the heart of a modern gallant has often room enough to accommodate half a dozen. The reason of which I conclude to be, that either the hearts of the gentlemen have grown larger, or the persons of the ladies smaller: this, however, is a question for physiologists to determine.

Wit is a device for producing laughter or amusement by means of an unexpected but pertinent association of apparent incongruities. Wit may, or may not, include laughter, but it strives for novelty, surprise, and intellectual brilliance. Its distinguishing marks are individuality in point of view, ingenuity, and critical subtlety. Its favorite sphere is the realm of ideas. In mood it is pungent, sharply critical, and at times even cruel. Wit appears in many guises, but the following will illustrate several of its varieties:

To do him justice, he appears to have as much speculative benevolence as any private gentleman in the kingdom, though he is seldom so sensual as to indulge himself in the exercise of it.

(Sheridan, *The School for Scandal*)

Not louder shrieks to pitying Heaven are cast,
When husbands, or when lapdogs, breathe their last.
(Pope, *The Rape of the Lock*)

We were not fairly beaten, my lord. No Englishman is ever fairly beaten.

(Shaw, *St. Joan*)

Wit may consist of a play upon words or of the interplay of ideas. The simplest, also often referred to as the lowest, form of wit is the pun. A **pun** is the use of a word in more than one sense. It may be illustrated by a familiar story told about the artist Whistler, who enjoyed a reputation as a wit. In response to Whistler's boast that he could make a pun upon any subject, it was suggested that he make a pun upon the king. "Impossible," replied Whistler; "the king is no subject."

Under the heading of wit may be noted two specialized devices often associated with wit: epigram and paradox. **Epigram** is wit marked by an unexpected turn of the idea and by pithiness of expression. Two somewhat different examples are:

It is only the modern that ever becomes old-fashioned.
(Wilde, *The Decay of Lying*)

Ah, dear Marwood, what's integrity to an opportunity?
(Congreve, *The Way of the World*)

Paradox is wit which attempts to suggest subtly a new aspect of truth by means of a statement which is apparently either self-contradictory or contradictory of common sense or generally accepted fact. A classic example of paradox is the description of Lancelot's dilemma as he finds his devotion to the pure Elaine prevented by his guilty passion for Guinevere:

> And peradventure had he seen her first
> She might have made this and that other world
> Another world for the sick man; but now
> The shackles of an old love straighten'd him,
> *His honor rooted in dishonor stood,*
> *And faith unfaithful kept him falsely true.*
> (Tennyson, *Lancelot and Elaine*)

Of the more extended and complex devices, the most important are known as satire and burlesque. Both satire and burlesque have a common method and purpose: namely, the coupling of criticism and ridicule. For this reason they frequently overlap. They differ, however, in the relative emphasis given to their component elements.

Satire is a device for achieving critical rejection or repudiation by means of ridicule. Its method is the presentation of its subject as incompatible with sound reason and therefore as either ludicrous or contemptible. The quality of its ridicule may vary from good-natured raillery to biting scorn. It should be noted, however, that the laughter of satire is never more than a means to an end—an end which is criticism and repudiation. Some distinguished satires are Dryden's *Absalom and Achitophel,* Pope's *Dunciad,* and Byron's *Don Juan,* as well as *Gulliver's Travels* by Swift, *A Connecticut Yankee in King Arthur's Court* by Mark Twain, and *Babbitt* by

Sinclair Lewis. Although satire is somewhat difficult to illustrate in brief compass, the following observation of Gulliver, when the King of Brobdingnag fails to grasp the cultural advantages of gunpowder, presents one aspect:

A strange effect of narrow principles and short views! that a prince possessed of every quality which procures veneration, love, and esteem; of strong parts, great wisdom, and profound learning, endued with admirable talents for government, and almost adored by his subjects, should from a nice unnecessary scruple, whereof in Europe we can have no conception, let slip an opportunity put into his hands, that would have made him absolute master of the lives, the liberties, and the fortunes of his people. Neither do I say this with the least intention to detract from the many virtues of that excellent king, whose character I am sensible will on this account be very much lessened in the opinion of an English reader: but I take this defect among them to have risen from their ignorance, they not having hitherto reduced politics into a science, as the more acute wits of Europe have done.

(Swift, *Gulliver's Travels*)

Burlesque (or **travesty**), on the other hand, is a device for provoking mirth by a critical reduction to absurdity of the inherent incongruities of its subject. Its origin is a critical sense of incongruity. Its method is that of emphasis and exaggeration. Its object is delight in the ludicrous. Burlesque is never bitter. In contrast to satire, it should be noted that its critical repudiation is but the means to its proper end, which is laughter. A famous example is the burlesque of amateur theatricals provided by the dramatic misadventures of Bottom and the artisans in Shakespeare's *A Midsummer Night's Dream*. Since burlesque derives its point from that which is burlesqued and since it frequently deals with subjects of passing interest, most burlesque is likely to be ephemeral. Some notable burlesques which have survived, however, are Pope's *Rape of the Lock,* Gay's *The Beggars' Opera,* and many of the Gilbert and Sullivan light operas.

A device closely akin to satire and burlesque, but applied particularly to works of literature, is known as parody. **Parody** is a device for implying criticism by means of selective imitation, exaggeration, and mild ridicule. The subject of parody is usually some familiar work of literature. Its method is the careful selection and duplication of the characteristic mannerisms, attitudes, and ideas of such a work, an exaggeration and emphasis of them, and a consequent reduction of them to absurdity. Its object is to provide amusement through the skill and justice of the criticism inherent in its method. The following satiric jibe at Wordsworth is a clever parody of that poet's *She Dwelt Among the Untrodden Ways:*

> He lived amidst th' untrodden ways
>   To Rydal Lake that lead;
> A bard whom there were none to praise,
>   And very few to read.
>
> Behind a cloud his mystic sense,
>   Deep hidden, who can spy?
> Bright as the night when not a star
>   Is shining in the sky.
>
> Unread his works—his "Milk White Doe"
>   With dust is dark and dim;

It's still in Longman's shop, and oh!
The difference to him!
(*Attributed to* Hartley Coleridge)

A specialized extension of satire is known as invective.
Invective is a device for attaining condemnation by
means of explicit denunciation. It is satire minus the
laughter. Its usual method is savage ridicule and excoria-
tion designed to render its subject contemptible. A brief
example of the manner and mood of invective is Hamlet's
speech to Ophelia:

Get thee to a nunnery, go. Farewell! Or, if thou wilt needs
marry, marry a fool; for wise men know well enough what
monsters you make of them. To a nunnery, go, and quickly,
too. Farewell! . . . I have heard of your paintings, too, well
enough. God has given you one face, and you make your-
selves another. You jig, you amble, and you lisp and nick-
name God's creatures and make your wantonness your ignorance. Go to, I'll no more on't; it hath made me mad.

(Shakespeare, *Hamlet*)

[The terms given to the devices listed above, it should be
noted, are, by transference, also applied to the product which
results from their use. Thus the terms *humor, wit, satire,
burlesque, travesty, parody,* and *invective* refer both to the
respective methods employed and the literary result of the
method.]

One final device, which involves both comparison and
contrast, which to a certain extent implies criticism, but
which does not include laughter and is otherwise somewhat apart from the foregoing, is known as pastoralism.
Pastoralism is a means of ornamenting, emphasizing,
and idealizing certain aspects of life: (1) by assuming

that the essentials of human experience may be represented in a more simple, beautiful, and ideal form in the imaginary existence of conventionalized shepherds; and (2) by reinterpreting the circumstances of familiar life in terms of such an artificial existence. It is a device entirely arbitrary and conventionalized, and interprets life according to its own highly restricted criteria. The world which it creates is not intended to reproduce actuality. True to its original meaning (the term is derived from the Latin word for "shepherd"), it conventionalizes human nature into the rôles of shepherds and shepherdesses. Amid idyllic rural settings, it reduces all of human activity to the simple and tranquil pursuits of an idealized rusticity. This does not mean that pastoralism confines itself to sweetness and light. On the contrary, the shadow of sorrow or evil may fall across its green pastures and still waters, and the shepherd may lament over a broken reed. But in all it remains faithful to an idyllic artificiality, rebuilding actuality into a golden age of the imagination. The pastoral device is used in Spenser's group of poems, *The Shepherd's Calendar,* in Sir Philip Sidney's romance, *The Arcadia,* and in John Fletcher's play, *The Faithful Shepherdess.* Pastoralism has been particularly effective in elegaic poetry, as is evidenced by Milton's *Lycidas,* Shelley's *Adonais,* and Arnold's *Thyrsis.* When a work of literature, in either prose or verse, employs throughout the conventional devices of pastoralism, and particularly when it takes the form of a dialogue or song contest between shepherds, such a work is known formally as a **pastoral.** The following illustrates the pastoral manner:

Together both, ere the high lawns appeared
Under the opening eyelids of the morn,
We drove afield, and both together heard
What time the gray-fly winds her sultry horn,
Battening our flocks with the fresh dews of night,
Oft till the star that rose, at evening, bright
Toward Heaven's descent had sloped his westering wheel.
Meanwhile the rural ditties were not mute,
Tempered to the oaten flute;
Rough Satyrs danced, and Fauns with cloven heel
From the glad sound would not be absent long,
And old Damœtas loved to hear our song.

(Milton, *Lycidas*)

CHAPTER III

THE TYPES OF LITERATURE: THE ESSAY

As we have seen, that kind of art which we call creative literature is a verbal interpretation of life by an artist. The general means of giving artistry to this verbal interpretation of life are the technical devices which have just been discussed. But these technical devices lend themselves to a variety of combinations, and thus may produce a number of different effects. For example, the means of presenting his interpretation which are available to the artist—description, narration, exposition, and argumentation—are common to all literary expression. But they may appear in different combinations with varying degrees of emphasis in such a manner as to serve different purposes and create different effects. These different purposes and effects are associated with several generally recognized types of literature.

The types of creative literature depend upon the general method chosen by a literary artist to express his interpretation of life. Specifically, the artist may choose to present his interpretation either directly or indirectly. The direct method is simply a straightforward explanation of his views by the artist, addressing the reader directly and speaking in his own person. To convey his interpretation indirectly, he has three courses open to him. He may embody his interpretation of life in a story. He may give a mimetic representation of it. Or he may attempt to suggest it sensuously and emotionally by means of symbol, imagery, and music.

When the literary artist endeavors to express his interpretation of life by constructing a story which will embody it, the type of literature which results is known as *fiction*. When he chooses the method of mimetic representation, the resultant type is called *drama*. When he chooses the sensuous implications of symbol, imagery, and music, the result is called *poetry*. It must be understood that these three methods are not mutually exclusive. They are very closely allied, and, as we shall see, often merge one with another. But beyond these there exist no possible methods whereby the literary artist can convey his interpretation of life indirectly.

The direct method of interpretation results in only one generally recognized and pure type of creative literature. This is known as the *essay*. The essay, as its name implies, is a composition in prose or verse, usually rather brief, which *essays*, or attempts, to interpret life by explaining a personal reaction to some item, or items, of experience. Like the other types of literature, it may use freely any of the mechanical devices of presentation and appeal. It may employ narration, description, exposition, or argumentation as it finds need. But always it does so for the purpose of explaining directly to the reader the personal views of the author.

Of all literary types, the essay is perhaps the most elastic. It is permitted the greatest freedom of style and method. Strictly speaking, it is formless; or, rather, its forms are as numerous as the ingenuity of the artist can devise. Although usually brief, it may vary widely in both scope and length. It may range from a brief comment to so lengthy an interpretation of life as Burton's expanded essay, *The Anatomy of Melancholy*.

The essay, however, must not be confused with certain writings which somewhat resemble it. Of such nature are the treatise, the thesis, and the so-called "article." These latter, in so far as they remain true to their character, are purely informative, impersonal, and objective in their exposition and interpretation. They are really, therefore, types of non-creative literature, while the essay is always personal and creative. In so far as these non-creative types may add personal and subjective touches to their interpretations of fact, they may rise to the level of creative literature, and, while remaining treatise, thesis, or article, they may approach the manner and treatment of the essay. Of such a nature are Bryce's *American Commonwealth* and Huxley's *The Physical Basis of Life*.

Of a somewhat different character are such literary types as biography, autobiography, history, diaries, and journals. Strictly speaking, these are all primarily records of facts, and therefore not creative literature at all. But each in its own way *may* be made a work of art. It may assume the qualities and technique of fiction, drama, or even poetry. Most frequently such types adopt the methods and manner of the essay. Of them it may, therefore, be said that, to the extent that they combine with their bare recital of facts the methods of fiction, drama, poetry, and essay, they invade the realm of creative literature. And to the extent that they include the personal reactions and interpretations, the manner and flavor, of the essay, they approximate the essay in effect. Thus Strachey's *Queen Victoria* and Adams's *The Education of Henry Adams* are good examples of a biography and an auto-biography which, using the methods of narrative, and often approaching fiction, essay the interpretation of per-sonalities. Carlyle's *French Revolution* and Macaulay's *History of England* add to a mere record of facts what is in effect a personal interpretation of the experience of the race. And such diaries and journals as those of Pepys and Evelyn become creative literature in the proportion that drama and personal revelation and interpreta-tion are superimposed upon the bald account of daily happenings. But since such types, when they are to be classed as creative literature, employ relatively simple methods of presentation and have little or no complex specialized technique, except that borrowed from other types, they do not require separate discussion.

It must be remembered, however, that, no matter how closely such types may approximate the essay, the essay itself is a separate and distinct type of creative literature. Relatively short, direct, individual, and interpretive, it is a frank and human disclosure of the impact of life upon a personality. It is readily identified. What makes defin-ing the essay difficult is the fact that, properly speaking, it has no form. Its superficial outlines are blurred and protean. Such form as it has is structural, not external but internal. And that structural form is the ordering of its component parts according to a logical arrangement.

Although the essay as such has no specific form, it often appears in a guise which lends it a semblance of form. Thus it may appear in the form of a dialogue, as in the dialogues of Plato, Dryden, or Franklin. Often it takes the form of an editorial, review, or similar journalistic comment. It may be cast in the conventionalized mould of the letter, as in the letters of James Howell, Horace Walpole, or Lord Chesterfield. Or it may be delivered orally in the form of an oration, speech, or sermon.

I. The Manner of the Essay

The field of the essay is vast, sprinkled with many strange flowers, each growing in its own individual way and pungent with its own perfume. It is this individuality of growth and of perfume, the flavor of personality, which creates the subtle bouquet of the essay style. In other words, the manner adopted by the essayist toward his reader is one of the most distinctive characteristics of the essay. This manner, as expressed in the structure and phraseology of the essay, may be either formal or informal, and results in two kinds of essays which may be classified similarly. Although there is no sharp line of demarcation between the two, they are subject to definition and are usually recognizable.

The **formal essay** is the interpretation of a personal reaction developed in accordance with an obvious structural pattern and expressed in formal or austere and dignified language. Like one among strangers the formal essayist withholds his full personality, remaining somewhat aloof and reserved. The structural pattern of his work is clear-cut and logical, and he rarely deviates from it. Thus the essays of Newman and Arnold are distinctly formal, while those of Swift and Stevenson are somewhat less so.

Let us consider as an illustration a modern formal essay, Aldous Huxley's *The Outlook for American Culture*. The author begins with an introduction designed to explain his choice of topic and method of developing it. He explains that the future of America is the future of the world, and then points out that the future can be predicted in terms of the present. For the purpose of his present prediction, he announces that he will consider three factors in their relation to culture. These are machinery, the American social and political organization, and education.

In the body of his essay, Huxley in turn discusses the first two factors, which converge inevitably, as he shows, upon the third. He enumerates the benefits of machinery as it creates opportunities for culture. On the other hand, he shows that each advantage is offset by a disadvantage inimical to culture. The most serious of these latter is the opportunity for capitalists to control culture.

This naturally leads to a consideration of the American social and political democracy. Once again Huxley balances the advantages and disadvantages, concluding that the success of democracy depends upon adequate education.

Since the two preceding considerations inevitably lead to the question of education, Huxley now discusses the fallacy of democratic education. This, he declares, is the assumption that everyone has the same capacity for culture. Disproving this, he insists that the education of the future must be an education adapted to intellectual capacity.

His conclusion derives from the last conviction. Since, for the purpose of education, humanity must be divided into psychological types, he predicts a new social structure conforming to these types. It must also follow that the political organization will become a democracy of opportunity according to capacity: in reality, an aristocracy of culture. The inadequacy of the existing system, he insists, demands such a conclusion as its only possible remedy.

The formal structure of the essay is thus obvious. Each part adheres to a formal structural pattern, which is thrown into relief and which proceeds by logical transitions from point to point to build up a coherent whole. It may readily be digested into the form of an outline thus:

A. Introduction: explanation of the problem
B. Body of the discussion
    1. Machinery
        a. Benefits for culture
        b. Detriments to culture
    2. Social and political system
        a. Merits of democracy

     b. Deficiencies of democracy

     c. Dependence upon education

  3. Education

     a. Fallacy of democratic education

     b. Need for psychological realism

C. Conclusion

  1. Education demands division of mankind according to capacity

  2. Social classification must conform to this

  3. Democracy must give opportunity according to capacity

  4. These changes implicit in the failure of existing system

But in expression, too, the essay is formal. The writer does not assume the friendliness of his reception. He is courteous, urbane, but dignified. He asks no concessions to his personality, but stands upon the soundness of his thinking and the logic of its presentation. His manner is that of a man speaking to his equals, but yielding and expecting no more than is consistent with the decorum of good taste.

The **informal essay** is the interpretation of a personal reaction expressed in informal, or familiar and colloquial language, and conforming to no obvious structural pattern. The informal essayist is neither aloof nor dignified. Like one among friends, he says what he pleases, certain that no one will misunderstand or take offense. Although his work may have a hidden logic of its own, it will have no obvious structural pattern, and he may wander at will. Thus the essays of Addison, Lamb, and Holmes are distinctly informal, while those of Hazlitt and Thoreau are somewhat less so.

Consider, for example, Charles Lamb's *Old China* as an illustration of the informal manner in the essay. Structurally the essay follows a very informal pattern which is built, not upon a logical sequence of ideas, but upon a chain of mental associations. The author opens by confessing to "an almost feminine partiality for old china." Then, after a few pleasant, disconnected comments on the subject, he introduces the character of Bridget, his "cousin," as one who shares his enthusiasm. In recalling the joy they shared at a time when the acquisition of a new piece of china meant a serious strain on their finances, and even actual deprivation, he is led upon a digression which ranges far from his original subject. He reminisces about the past pleasures of poverty, when every little excursion was an inexpensive joy and every purchase a positive triumph. He compares the relative joys of poverty and wealth. At the end of his digression—which is really the body of the essay—he returns once more to the subject of old china, and we see that it has been merely a springboard for his real discussion.

Structurally this essay is informal because, although it has a pattern, that pattern is hidden and, moreover, is extremely loose and elastic. In expression, too, the essay is informal. The writer speaks directly to his reader in a pleasant conversational tone, commenting on a subject dear to his own heart with the full confidence that his reader, like an old friend, will be as interested in the subject as the writer is.

II. THE MATTER OF THE ESSAY

Although the matter of the essay is always the personal reactions of the essayist toward his subject, those reactions may be of two kinds. They may be simply impressions, or they may be reasoned judgments. Essays, therefore, may be classified as essays of impression and as essays of judgment. Both kinds of matter, however, are often found in varying degrees in a single essay.

Essays of impression are those which are made up chiefly of the essayist's personal impressions of himself, of other people, of the natural life about him, and of man-made products. The four commonly used terms for such essays are: the personal essay, the character essay, the descriptive essay, and the essay of appreciation.

The **personal essay** is composed of the essayist's impressions of his own personality, or of some separate trait or quality of his own. The essayist may discuss his own opinions, his prejudices, his likings, his moods, or his reminiscences. Almost invariably his manner is informal, and, usually, his purpose is to amuse. Thus Cowley's *Of Myself* is a pleasant analysis of the writer's personality, Montaigne's *Of the Education of Children* exploits the author's rather curious opinions of the subject, Max Beerbohm's *An Infamous Brigade* expresses an amusing prejudice against firemen, Hunt's *On Getting Up On Cold Mornings* exhibits a most unusual liking, while Lamb's *Christ Hospital* tells of memories of long ago, and his *Dream Children* reveals him in a mood of exquisite pathos.

The **character essay** is composed of impressions of other people. Frequently judgment may enter in, particularly in biography, an extension of the type. The character essay may deal with individuals, real or imaginary, with types, with groups or classes of people, or with a generalized trait of character. For example, the Earl of Clarendon gives his impressions of Charles I in his *History of the Rebellion,* Addison and Steele, in various papers from *The Spectator,* present an amusing portrait of the imaginary Sir Roger de Coverley, Earle somewhat critically analyses a type in *A Young Gentleman of the University,* Gelett Burgess mingles judgment with impressions in *Bromides and Sulfites* to picture general traits of character, and H. W. Nevinson gives his impressions of the whole United States in his *Good-bye, America.*

The **descriptive essay** is composed of impressions of a scene, natural or the product of mankind. The essayist describes and explains what has meaning to him: birds and animals, a cloud, a river, a street, a building, or a city. So the naturalist Beebe pictures the wild life of the jungle in *Jungle Peace,* Ruskin gains impressions of beauty and meaning from the sky and running water in *Modern Painters,* Simeon Strunsky writes of Broadway in *The Street,* Irving pictures *Bracebridge Hall* for us, and Goldsmith presents us with whimsical impressions disguised as *A Chinese View of London.*

The **essay of appreciation** is composed of impressions of the skill and art which man has achieved in the making of things. Generally, judgment and approval have preceded the appreciation, and the essayist is concerned only with recording his impressions, "the adventures of his soul among masterpieces." His subject is usually some specific work of art, a painting, a poem, a play, and the like. Occasionally it may be extended to include the maker for the sake of what he has made. For example, Pater records his impressions of a famous painting in *La Gioconda,* Lamb voices his approval of *The Artificial Comedy of the Last Century,* and Morley pays tribute to a famous teacher in *In Memoriam—Francis Barton Gummere.*

On the whole, essays of this type are favorable to the subjects considered. Occasionally, however, the impressions they record may be unfavorable, as in Lamb's *Imperfect Sympathies* or Hazlitt's *On Disagreeable People.*

Essays of judgment are those which are made up chiefly of the essayist's reasoned conclusions upon a variety of subjects of sufficient importance to deserve careful analysis and impartial evaluation. These subjects may be man-made things, natural things, or ultimates. According to the choice of subject, the resultant essay is known respectively as critical, scientific, or philosophical.

The **critical essay** is composed of judgments upon the tangible and intangible products of society, from a work of art to a specific institution or aspect of the social scene. The judgment expressed is the result of a logical evaluation of the subject, usually in the light of a predetermined standard of values. Johnson's *Life of Addison* and Jeffrey's essay on Wordsworth's *Excursion* are judgments of the work of artists, while Arnold's *Hebraism and Hellenism* and Aldous Huxley's *The Outlook for American Culture* are judgments upon specific aspects of society.

The **scientific essay** is composed of judgments upon the phenomena of nature and their relations to humanity. Such essays are more than impressions of the superficial aspects of things; they deal, rather, with the findings of modern science about those innumerable elements, their groupings and blendings according to natural laws, which, taken in the aggregate, are known as nature. For example, Thomas Huxley judicially examines the miracle we know simply as *A Piece of Chalk,* Sir J. A. Thomson analyses, describes, and evaluates *The New World of Science,* and Robert A. Millikan puts together and interprets judicially certain discoveries about *Available Energy* which "may constitute an important and perpetually burning beacon to point out to mankind the way of progress."

The **philosophical essay** is composed of judgments upon ultimates, that is, upon those theories, ideas, or concepts underlying the phenomena of all life. Usually reflective and serious in tone, the philosophical essay represents the judgment of a mature wisdom, of a mind ripened by the sober contemplation of life's many facets. Upon whatever subject the philosophical essayist turns his gaze—literature, education, morals, religion, social relationships, or life itself—he seeks to pierce through the *thing* to its essence, its ultimate reality. This essence, defined, weighed, evaluated, becomes the subject for his essay. For example, Pater defines two concepts of the literary art in *Classic and Romantic;* Newman deals with the essence of the educative process, its methods and values, in his *Idea of a University;* Havelock Ellis strips the veneer from conventional morality and shows us the underlying reality in his *The Art of Morals* (in *The Dance of Life*); Sir Thomas Browne surveys his own concepts of religion, and, in so doing, surveys all concepts, in *Religio Medici;* Emerson discusses the realities of human relationships, and the relations of man to God in *Self-Reliance;* and Stevenson seeks—and, to his own satisfaction, finds—the reality, the ultimate beneath all life, and interprets this reality in *Aes Triplex.*

CHAPTER IV

THE TYPES OF LITERATURE: FICTION

As we have seen in the preceding chapter, one of the ways by which an artist can give creative expression to his interpretation of life is the presentation of a story which embodies it. To this type of creative literature is given the name fiction. Now the telling of a story is one of the most rudimentary and popular kinds of human entertainment. But not all telling of stories is an art, nor is all artistic narrative fiction.

Art in narrative implies a technique of arrangement and presentation which will give to narrative beauty of form and execution and unity of effect. But this artistic finish may be given to a story of actual happenings, to, in other words, a narrative dominated by fact. Such are history and biography. And narrative of this sort must be distinguished from fiction.

Fiction is a product of the creative imagination. Like all literary art, it is rooted in human experience; but the distinguishing mark of fiction is the transmutation which it makes of that experience. Upon the welter of human experience it imposes a pattern. It selects, omits, arranges the items of experience until a design can be seen to emerge. This design is presented as a narrative, based upon human experience, incorporating it, and yet differing from it in that it represents life ordered and rendered meaningful according to the artist's interpretation.

Thus fiction is the literary account of imaginary persons and imaginary events in an artistically imaginative world. Depending upon the purposes of the artist, that imaginative world may approach closely or recede from the realm of actual human experience. But it should be noted that the purpose of fiction is never to provide a mere record of reality; its purpose is to create artificially an illusion of reality. It represents the spectacle of life as seen through the interpreting eyes of the artist.

The primary purpose of fiction is the study of human nature in the concrete. But attendant upon this are the equally important purposes of entertainment, stimulation, and even instruction. In achieving these purposes, fiction may be either serious or light in tone; but, whether serious or light, it remains an artistic interpretation of life. It is only when, through carelessness or wilful perversion, fiction distorts or falsifies its picture of life, that its art becomes dishonest and forfeits its claim to serious consideration. Great and enduring fiction is invariably to be distinguished by intellectual honesty, interpretive seriousness, and artistic integrity.

But even when marked by these characteristics, fiction may vary according to the attitude of the writer toward his material. As we saw in the first chapter, a writer may view the raw material of his art realistically or romantically. When his personal bias is realistic, he will endeavor to create in his fiction an illusion of average normal human experience. Such fiction is described as *realistic*. When, on the other hand, the peculiar qualities of the romantic attitude combine to create an illusion which is the antithesis of common human experience, the result is what is known as *romance*. Without any substantial difference in its elements or its technique, the novel, for example, may be either realistic or romantic. Thus Howells's story of New England, *The Rise of Silas Lapham,* may be called a realistic novel, while Hawthorne's tale of New England, *The Scarlet Letter,* is a romantic novel or romance.

In addition, different kinds of fiction are often classified in terms of their subject matter. Thus the historical novel, like Reade's *The Cloister and the Hearth,* is concerned primarily with a recreation of the past. The adventure story, like Stevenson's *Treasure Island,* concentrates upon thrilling exploits in settings conducive to abundant action. The love story (or "romance," as it is frequently called), like Blackmore's *Lorna Doone,* is concerned with the romantic, and usually idealized, journeys which end in lovers' meeting. The mystery story, like Conan Doyle's *The Hound of the Baskervilles,* propounds a riddle, usually associated with crime, and devotes itself to the solution. And the horror story, like Bram Stoker's *Dracula,* exploits the supernatural and the terrifying for the deliberate production of gooseflesh.

All these kinds of fiction, however, are determined by the subject matter or the attitude of the writer. They differ very little in fundamental technique. Such technical differences as they reveal are to a certain extent caused by the nature of the story, but in the main are determined by quite another factor. For the objectives of each of these fictional types may be attained in a number of ways, depending upon the writer's purpose and the particular effect he desires. The means of achieving these different effects constitute the technique of fiction, and the combination of their various devices and methods results in the recognized fictional forms. To the discussion of these the remainder of this chapter is devoted.

I. THE ELEMENTS OF FICTION

Every story, whether fictitious or factual, is bound to consist of certain definite elements. These correspond to three questions which inevitably arise in connection with any narrative: Who participated in the events? What happened? And where and under what circumstances did it happen? In other words, every story must take into account the persons involved, what they do or what is done to them, and the general situation. Similarly no fictitious story can be properly effective without due attention to these elements. To these three elements of fiction are given the technical names, respectively, of character, plot, and setting.

But although all three elements are inevitably present in every work of fiction, it must be understood that they may vary widely in relative importance and emphasis. Thus it may suit the purpose of one writer to devote most of his attention and emphasis to the study of character, with the result that his work is often described as character fiction. With another, the story may be the thing; and the product of this interest is what is often called the action story. Or occasionally it is the setting which is given pre-eminence, and there results the story of environment, local color, or atmosphere. Moreover each of these elements may be given different kinds of development and may be devoted to different purposes according to the artistic intention of the writer. For these reasons it is well to consider them in some detail.

CHARACTERS

Characters are the people who appear in a story. They may be drawn from history; they may be replicas of people the author has known; or they may be pure figments of the imagination. Furthermore, they may be ordinary human beings, supernatural creatures, animals, or even personifications of ideas or natural forces.

The nature, as well as the artistic value, of fictional characters is determined by two considerations, one quantitative and the other functional. The first is concerned with the question: How much is it desirable for one to know about a given character? The second is concerned with the use to which a character is put in the story. Of course both considerations are intimately related, but for the sake of clarity let us examine them separately.

Some characters it is desirable to know as completely and intimately as possible. Such a character is of interest as an individual, as a distinct personality separate from his fellows and peculiar to himself. His individuality is unique; he possesses an independent identity as distinctive and recognizable as that of an actual human being. Indeed, such a character often steps from the pages of a book and seems as real as if he had a genuine physical existence. On the other hand, for the immediate purpose it may be necessary to know only enough about a character to identify him with a familiar group or social attitude of which he may be a representative. For instance, if the only important fact about a character is that he is a sailor, it is necessary to know about that character only so much as will impress the fact that he is a typical sailor. There are also times when it is only a single trait of character, a mannerism or eccentricity, which is of consequence. At such times it is desirable to suppress everything else about a character in order that this single trait may be thrown into relief. Obviously, these considerations dictate *how much* a given character shall be developed. They also result in three recognized kinds of characters known respectively as individual characters, typical characters, and caricatures.

An **individual character** is a character who stands out from the generality of mankind by reason of the unique combination of personal characteristics which isolate him from his fellow men and emphasize his individuality. Thus in Mark Twain's *Huckleberry Finn,* Colonel Sherburn is a country gentleman of the South who has an individuality of his own. Individual also are Godfrey Cass, the young squire of George Eliot's *Silas Marner,* and Long John Silver, the piratical sailor of Stevenson's *Treasure Island.* Such characters, however, may be presented in either of two ways. They may be shown as either static or developing. A **static character** is one whose qualities, once set forth at the beginning of a story, do not change throughout the progress of the story. The characters of Cooper and Scott are usually of this kind. A **developing character,** however, is one in whom those qualities initially delineated upon his first appearance may be seen to undergo alteration under the influence of subsequent events, environment, or other characters. Of such a nature are the chief figures of Thackeray and Dickens, for example, Henry Esmond and Sidney Carton.

A **typical character** is one which represents a group or class. Within himself he sums up the salient characteristics of the group to which he belongs, while his chief value is his representation of the class which he typifies. Thus in any story may be found characters typical of a race, nation, or locality, of an occupation, or of a social attitude. For example, Colonel Grangerford, in *Huckleberry Finn,* is a typical Southern gentleman; the elder Squire Cass, of *Silas Marner,* is a typical English squire; and Captain Smollett, in *Treasure Island,* is a typical sailor.

A **caricature** is a character so developed as to be dominated by a single quality or characteristic. Naturally such development is neither well rounded nor complete, and is distorted by disproportionate emphasis. For this reason the caricature is never more than a partial portrait, one which is frequently eccentric and at times unreal and fantastic. Many examples may be found among the lesser characters of Dickens, such as Sairey Gamp, Scrooge, and Mr. Pecksniff.

But the **function of characters** also has much bearing

upon their nature and value. The function is the technical use to which a character is put in a story. This function cannot always be reduced to simple terms; for often a character performs more than one function. Nevertheless, although a character may have more than one use, it should be observed that the different functions still remain separate and distinct. Of these, the principal are those which follow.

The **protagonist** (a designation derived from the Greek: *protos,* first + *agonistes,* a contestant) is the leading character of the narrative. Usually the protagonist (who is sometimes called the "hero" or "heroine") is made the object of the reader's sympathy and approval. Whether this be true or not, it is the protagonist and his fortunes which enlist the chief interest of the reader. For example, in Scott's *Ivanhoe* the protagonist, for whom the reader's sympathy is sought, is Ivanhoe himself. Other characters in league with him—such as, in this case, Rowena, King Richard, Gurth, Wamba, and Rebecca—may be considered minor protagonists.

The **antagonist** (*anti,* against) is the character or force, internal or external, opposed to the protagonist. Ordinarily the reader is expected to desire the defeat of the antagonist and those characters in league with him. Examples of antagonists in *Ivanhoe* are Brian de Bois-Guilbert, Prince John, and De Bracy. The antagonist as an external natural force is found in Conrad's *Typhoon,* as Fate in Hardy's *The Return of the Native,* and as environment in Dreiser's *An American Tragedy.* The antagonist as internal force is exemplified in Austen's

Pride and Prejudice, in which the pride of Darcy and the prejudice of Elizabeth Bennett are opposed to the happiness of the couple.

The **foil** character is one whose personality is used to supplement and illuminate the personality of a more important character to whom the foil is subordinated. For example, Mulvaney, in Kipling's *Soldiers Three,* has two foils, his friends Ortheris and Learoyd. In Hawthorne's *The Scarlet Letter* Chillingworth is a foil for his character opposite, Dimmesdale.

The **confidant** is a character closely related to, but less important than, a major character. His use is, primarily, as one to whom the major character can reveal himself in conversation. Thus Dr. Watson is the confidant of Sherlock Holmes in Conan Doyle's famous stories. He is also, as it happens, the narrator. A similar double function is enjoyed by the unknown "I," narrator of Poe's *The Murders in the Rue Morgue.*

The **narrator** is simply the character who tells the story, if the narrative is written in the first person. He may be the protagonist, a minor figure, or even one who plays no part in the story at all. The narrator of Stevenson's *Treasure Island* is a protagonist, Jim Hawkins; the narrator of Poe's *The Gold Bug* is an unknown who has no function in the story except that of confidant; the narrator of Blackmore's *Lorna Doone* is the chief protagonist, John Ridd.

Background characters are those who appear in the story but are of little or no importance to the action. They may be utilized as expositors, as sources of comedy or pathos, as influences upon more important characters, or as aids in the development of an atmosphere of reality. Usually they are typical characters. For example, Governor Bellingham and the Reverend John Wilson are background characters in Hawthorne's *The Scarlet Letter*.

These are the principal kinds of characters and the uses to which they are put. The question now arises: How is the reader made acquainted with the characters of fiction? There are two **methods of character exposition.** The author may tell the reader directly all he needs to know about a character, or he may present the character in such a manner that the character himself gradually reveals what it is necessary to know about him. These two methods are known respectively as the explicit and the implicit methods.

The **explicit method** of character exposition permits the writer to explain his characters objectively, to study and analyze them for the benefit of the reader. This he may do either by means of separate expository essays, or by a sustained process of progressive analysis. The **essay method** of exposition, as its name implies, is one in which the author interrupts the even flow of the narrative to give directly his personal explanation and interpretation of the qualities of his characters. This is the method of Fielding in *Tom Jones,* and, in some degree, of Hawthorne in *The Scarlet Letter*. For instance, Chapter VI of the latter novel is, in effect, a complete essay characterizing the child, Pearl. The **method of progressive analysis,** on the other hand, does not break the narrative for the sake of expository excursions, but strews the course of the story with a running commentary of analysis and explanation upon the motives and reactions of the characters. This is the method of Eliot in *Silas Marner* and of Stevenson in such a psychological study as *Markheim*.

The **implicit method** of character exposition is that by which the nature of a figure in fiction is revealed through his own speeches and actions, through the comments and attitudes of other characters, and through the environment in which he lives. It is sometimes referred to as the dramatic method. This is the method of Mark Twain in *Huckleberry Finn* and *Tom Sawyer,* and of Dumas in *The Three Musketeers.*

PLOT

The second element of which fiction is composed is known as the plot. The plot (or, as it is sometimes called, the *fable*) of a narrative is the outline of action. It is the ordered sequence of events which forms the framework of the story. Regularly it consists of four structural elements.

The **structural elements** of a plot are known as exposition, involution, climax, and resolution. **Exposition** in fiction is the explanation of events or circumstances not given detailed presentation in the story. Since this explanation is often necessary for a full understanding of the situation with which the story opens, it is usually given at or near the beginning; but further explanation may appear later in the story as need arises. The **involution** (from the Latin, *in,* in + *volvo,* roll) is the winding together, or complication, of the threads of the plot leading to the climax. It is sometimes called by the cognate French term, the *nouement*. The **climax** is the high point of action at which the involution has reached its maximum complexity and demands a decisive settlement one way or another. In it the conflict of protagonist and antagonist comes to a head and the issue is determined. Subsidiary episodes of a plot may also have their climaxes, which direct the course of the complication and prepare for the major climax. Such a climax, which may occur at any point in the involution, may be called a minor climax. The major climax usually comes near the close of the story. The **resolution** (from the Latin, *re,* again + *solvo,* loosen) is the untangling of the threads of the plot after the climax. It brings the narrative to the conclusion implied by the climax, and usually it is fairly brief. This element is often referred to as the *dénouement*.

These elements of plot, however, may be combined in accordance with two different structural schemes. The structure of a plot may be either episodic or organic. An **episodic plot** is so called because the narrative consists of a number of parts, or episodes, each complete in itself, and connected with those episodes which precede or follow it only by a common character or group of characters. For example, Fielding's *Tom Jones,* Defoe's *Robinson Crusoe,* and Twain's *Huckleberry Finn* are episodic in structure. The **organic plot,** on the other hand, is so called because each event is causally related to the preceding and succeeding events, and the whole development of the plot is governed by the logic of cause and effect in human actions. Of such organic structure are Thackeray's *Henry Esmond,* Howells's *The Rise of Silas Lapham,* and Lewis's *Babbitt.*

A final factor which enters into plot is known as tempo. **Tempo** is the speed with which a narrative seems to move. Now tempo is a matter of psychological rather than physical time. It is determined largely by the nature of the selected incidents, their emotional weight and emphasis. Although tempo may vary somewhat within any given narrative, the total effect, according to the author's purpose, will be seen to conform with one of three recognized tempos: the normal tempo of life, retarded tempo, or accelerated tempo.

Normal tempo is that which endeavors to give the illusion of reality and immediacy. The narrative which may be said to move with normal tempo imitates the rhythm of life itself, preserving a nice balance between action and non-action, between intensity of experience and dullness. Thus the tempo of Eliot's *Middlemarch* or of Lewis's *Babbitt* approximates that of normal life. **Retarded tempo** is that of a narrative which seems to move with less than the speed of normal life. Action is reduced, and such action as remains is drawn out by a deliberate and lengthy dwelling upon fine points of motive and character reaction. Thus Richardson's *Clarissa Harlowe* and James's *The Ambassadors* are developed in retarded tempo. **Accelerated tempo** is that of a narrative which seems to move very swiftly. This effect is achieved usually through the emphasis given to action and the close sequence of incidents. Such tempo appears in Stevenson's *Treasure Island* or *The Black Arrow,* and in Dumas's *The Three Musketeers.*

The third element of fiction is setting. Setting is the sum total of all the tangible and intangible factors which the writer combines to form a background for his characters and their actions. These factors may be physical, including both natural phenomena and the creations of man. To the former class belong the earth, its oceans, mountains, animals, and vegetation; to the latter, the cities, homes, factories, and all normal appurtenances which are the traces of human habitation. On the other hand, these factors may be mental. Of this sort are the traditions, customs, manners, habits of thought, and conventional beliefs which form the intangible background of intellectual beings.

According to the intent of the writer and the factors he selects, the setting in fiction may be used in three ways. As simply a **pictorial background,** physical setting provides a theatre for the action and gives, as it were, "to airy nothing a local habitation and a name." It may be used to supply an air of reality to a story, or merely to add decorative touches. In Defoe's *Robinson Crusoe,* for example, the effect of the setting is both decorative and factually realistic. In some fiction this kind of setting is used primarily to throw into relief the distinctive characteristics of a specific locality. When so used, physical setting is often referred to as **local color.**

Setting may be used, also, as an **environmental force.**

That is, in either its physical or mental aspect, it may be shown to exert an influence upon characters and even to affect the development of the plot. This modifying force, of course, may vary widely; but sometimes it is treated as the greatest single agent in the development of the story. It is so used in Hardy's *The Return of the Native* and Hawthorne's *The Great Stone Face.*

Setting, finally, may be used to create atmosphere. **Atmosphere** in fiction is more than pictorial background, and may be more or less than environmental force. It is a very elusive quality and one rather difficult to describe. Setting which creates atmosphere is setting which establishes an emotional tone appropriate to the characters and circumstances of the story. In this way setting becomes a re-enforcement of the meaning of the narrative, and enhances its emotional significance. Obvious examples of this kind of setting are to be found in many of the stories of Poe, notably *The Fall of the House of Usher* and *The Masque of the Red Death,* or in Kipling's *The Man Who Would Be King.*

II. THE ART OF FICTION

In the preceding section we have examined the elements of which fiction is composed, and we have seen how those elements may be variously developed or treated to fit the purpose of the writer. When we come, however, to look at any example of a finished, well-told story, we are faced with the question: What makes the telling of this story effective? This is a further question of technique, for its answer is, in effect, dependent upon four qualities of good, or effective, narrative art. These qualities are: the selection of the material of which the story is composed, the arrangement of that material for the greatest effectiveness, the point of view from which the author has chosen to view his material, and the manner which he has adopted toward his reader. Each of these is sufficiently important to deserve elaboration.

In any art, **selection** implies the choice of that which is pertinent to the artist's purpose, and the elimination of all extraneous matter. By application, then, a well-told story contains only that material which is pertinent to the artist's purpose. However, in fiction, this selection is practiced in accord with certain principles, which may be called, roughly, the principles of length, breadth, and depth.

In other words, any well-told story may present a lengthwise, or longitudinal, section from life. Such a section has continuity in time and action, that is to say, length of duration; but, since it includes only one main action or series of actions, it has little breadth; and, since it deals only slightly, if at all, with the psychology of character, it has little depth. Such fiction usually includes stories dominated by plot, but the story which presents the progressive development of a character or the revelation of a setting, may also present a lengthwise section.

On the other hand, a story may present a lateral or breadthwise section of life, a section lacking in the continuity of time and events, but showing the complex interrelation of many people and many situations existing at the same time, much as a microtomic cross-section of a plant stem shows the complex structure of that stem. Obviously this principle is best seen in the contemporary impressionistic novel, but it appears also in its broadest use in such a series of novels, each of which has length, breadth, and depth, as Balzac's *Comédie Humaine*.

Finally, the well-told story may present a depthwise section. This depthwise section is, in effect, an analysis of the intricate details of the psychology of life. It is rarely found alone; yet, by its very nature, such exploration of the inner depths of psychology precludes much movement longitudinally, nor can it include much of a cross-section of life. Consequently it will be found that stories dominated by character are based mainly upon the principle of depth. The novels of Henry James are undoubtedly based upon a depthwise sectioning, but later writers have found even greater depths than he explored. Consequently we have to-day what has been called the "stream of consciousness" novel, in which whatever passes through the consciousness of a character, and sometimes even everything of which he is aware, becomes the material of the story. This principle of selection is illustrated in such contemporary novels as those of James Joyce and Virginia Woolf.

The second quality of a well-told story is the **arrangement** of its selected materials in such a manner as to make the most effective impression upon the reader. Unlike a picture, which makes its total effect almost instantaneously, a story can produce its total effect only by a progressive revelation of its parts. Consequently, it will be found that any well-told story has its material so arranged that it will arouse, maintain, and finally satisfy the reader's interest. This may be accomplished in various ways. The story may open with the exposition of characters or events, with description of setting, with the beginning of consecutive narrative, or even with the resolution of the story. Possibly the most effective opening, however, is that "in medias res" (in the middle of things), by which the reader is carried directly into the action of the story, with the necessary exposition of plot, setting, and character given in a following section.

In any well-told story it will be found that the reader's interest is maintained by suspense. **Suspense,** achieved by the arrangement of the selected materials, is the reader's uncertainty about the outcome of the plot, or the complete nature of the character to be revealed, or the total meaning of the atmosphere, or setting, which is gradually built up. As the design in a picture holds together and gives interest to that picture, so suspense in fiction holds together and maintains interest in the story.

It will be found further that, in any well-told story, the reader's interest, which has been aroused by the beginning of the story and maintained by suspense, will be satisfied at the end. This satisfaction comes about as the result of the reader's perception of the total meaning of the story, whether that meaning be explicit at the end of the story, or implicit in the completed pattern.

The third quality of a well-told story is the **point of view** from which the writer tells his story. In any story the material is presented according to certain well-defined principles. Specifically, the story may be told from the point of view of a narrator who stands either within or without the limits of the action. That is, the point of view may be either internal or external.

The first of these, the **internal point of view,** is that of a writer who tells his story in the first person, as though a participant in the action. As a means of carrying out this point of view consistently and effectively, he employs the device of assuming the personality of a character in the story. This personality may be that of the leading character, that of a secondary or minor figure, or that of a series of characters, each personality being assumed in turn.

The point of view of the chief character permits the direct narration of only those events in which that character has figured, and it permits the analysis of only one mind, the speaker's. For example, John Ridd, narrator of Blackmore's *Lorna Doone,* and Henry Esmond, narrator of Thackeray's *Henry Esmond,* can tell the reader only what they themselves see, know, do, feel, or think. The point of view of a secondary character similarly limits the narrative to only those events in which the character has figured; but because of his relative detachment from the main plot, the secondary character can be permitted to speak, as it were, for the author, to comment, to analyze, and to explain with authority. Thus in the Sherlock Holmes stories, Dr. Watson, as a minor participator in the events he chronicles, imparts to them through his comments a sense of immediate reality difficult to achieve otherwise. Similarly the "I" who tells the story of Poe's

The Fall of the House of Usher is able to comment and analyze freely because of his relative detachment from the plot. When, however, a writer assumes a number of personalities, his story is told from what may be termed a composite point of view. That is, the events of the story are viewed from several angles, and their total effect is achieved through the contributions of a number of major and minor figures, each adding his characteristic bit to the whole. Since this point of view presents, in effect, the illusion of a police-court summary of evidence, it is particularly effective in stories of crime and mystery. Wilkie Collins's *The Moonstone* and Browning's long narrative poem *The Ring and the Book* are good examples. It is further exemplified in many "epistolary novels," in which the story is told through letters between two or more characters in the action.

The **external point of view** is that of a writer who tells his story in the third person, from without the limits of the action. That is, he in no way identifies himself with the circumstances of his fiction, but speaks frankly as the author. As author, he is therefore responsible for the whole story, and his knowledge of it may be presumed to be all-inclusive. But voluntarily he may choose to affect a limitation of that knowledge. According to the degree that he does so, the point of view from which his story is told may be described as omniscient, limited, or detached.

The omniscient point of view is that of a writer who assumes god-like knowledge of his characters and of the events of the story. He may look at will into the mind of any character; he may observe and record whatever goes on at any time. This is the point of view of Hardy in *The Return of the Native,* of Scott in *Ivanhoe* or *The Talisman,* and of Meredith in *The Ordeal of Richard Feverel.* The limited point of view is that of a writer who limits his knowledge to a single character, analyzing and explaining that character and his actions fully, and showing other characters and events always in their relationship to his chosen character. For example, Jane Austen, in *Pride and Prejudice,* limits herself to the direct study of Elizabeth Bennett, and Dickens, in *A Christmas Carol,* tells his story always in relation to Scrooge. The detached point of view, however, differs somewhat from the two preceding. When writing from this point of view, the writer restricts himself to the presentation of only those external facts of character and action which may be discerned by a detached observer. Of the inner workings of his creations he attempts no explanation, but allows the observed and recorded phenomena to speak for themselves. This is the method, usually, of Maupassant, particularly in *A Piece of String;* and contemporary examples may be found in the work of Ernest Hemingway, notably *The Killers.*

The fourth quality of a well-told story is the **manner** the writer assumes toward his reader. This manner, or tone, depends upon the intrusion or suppression of the author himself as an audible interpreter of, or commentator upon, the material of the story. Obviously, in narratives written from the internal point of view or from the external detached point of view the author's person-

ality cannot enter openly into the story. In narratives
written from either the omniscient or the limited point
of view the author is at liberty to choose between two
manners: the personal and the impersonal. The personal,
or intrusive, manner is that of an author who comments
freely upon the actions and personalities of his characters, rejoicing audibly over their successes, sorrowing
over their failures, and generally setting forth his personal reactions to the circumstances of the story. This is
the manner of Thackeray and Fielding in most of their
work. The impersonal, or epic, manner is that of the
author who holds himself aloof from his reader, presenting his interpretation of life only indirectly through the
materials of his story. This is the manner adopted by
most modern writers.

III. FORM IN FICTION

It may be taken as almost axiomatic that, in any art,
the more resistant and restricted the medium of expression, the less latitude the artist is likely to have in adapt-
ing it to forms which will embody his interpretation of
life. As we have seen in our earlier discussion, the essay,
expressed in the fluid medium of words alone, encounters
so little formal restriction that the writer is confined to
no prescribed form. We shall see, however, that verse
and the theatre, the general media of expression in poetry
and the drama, inevitably impose certain restrictions upon
form. Fiction, circumscribed by relatively few restrictions
in medium, has in general more regularity of form than
the essay, but considerably less than poetry or the drama.

Such form as fiction may be said to possess is largely prescribed by two important factors. One is the scope of the particular work of fiction. The other is the fact that it is a work of art, and as such is designed to produce a unified effect. This necessity for unity of effect is really the key to form in fiction. But since it is intimately bound up with the matter of scope, it is better to examine the effect of scope first.

Scope, roughly defined, is the extent of the material treated by a work of fiction. It is a factor pertinent in all types of literature and all works of art. Thus the mere bulk of an essay, poem, play, or work of fiction, is determined by the scope of the material with which the writer deals, whether that material be ideas, emotions, or concrete realities, factual or imagined. For example, a story which deals with a panoramic cross-section of many actions, or with the total events in the life of a single individual, is necessarily of larger proportions than a story which deals with a single, sharply limited incident. Similarly a story which deals with both action and thought, with a minimum of selection—which has, in short, length, breadth, and depth—must be of greater bulk than a story which is limited to selected actions and thoughts, or which has length and breadth only.

Scope, therefore, both directly and indirectly has much to do with the form of fiction. For not only does it dictate the relative size of works of fiction, but, as bulk inevitably increases the complexity of fiction, scope also affects the means of maintaining a unity of effect. Since, however, the necessity of producing a unified effect remains constant in all works of fiction regardless of bulk, it is principally scope which serves as the distinguishing factor in differentiating the specialized forms which fiction assumes. These range from the brief, simple, and obvious unity of the anecdote, through a graduated series of more elaborate forms, to the large, complex, and less obvious unity of the novel. The generally recognized forms, as determined by scope, are those which follow.

The **anecdote** is a very short bit of narrative, frequently humorous, illustrative of some quality of human nature, either universal or applied to a specific individual. Its structure is usually climactic and pointed, so that when the "nub," or point, of the story is told the application becomes self-evident. Examples may be found among the numerous anecdotes that have been told of famous men, particularly the story of Washington and the cherry tree, or the anecdote told by Franklin in *The Whistle*.

The **short short-story,** a recently popularized form, is not usually, as its name implies, a shortened, or compressed, short-story. It presents an incident or event, is sharply climactic in structure, and with all other elements subordinated to that of plot. Journalistic in style, it aims more to surprise the reader than to edify him. Kipling's earlier stories, particularly *His Wedded Wife,* are good examples of the short short-story, as are many of the stories of Richard Harding Davis, particularly *The Hungry Man Was Fed*.

The **narrative sketch,** in reality an impressionistic essay employing the methods of fiction, purposes to present a cross-section of life, or to develop a mood or a character, and is often only a part of a longer work. Irving's *Sketch-Book* contains many such short, narrative sketches, notably *The Stout Gentleman* and *The Stage Coach*.

The **tale** is a brief fictitious narrative written in a leisurely manner and lacking in compression and conscious unity of effect. It purposes merely to tell a short, simple story in an artless, straightforward way. Such stories as Irving's *Rip Van Winkle*, Hawthorne's *Young Goodman Brown*, or the stories from *The Arabian Nights* are to be classified as tales rather than as short-stories.

The **short-story** is a short fictitious narrative which presents its materials with the greatest possible economy of means in order to produce a unified effect as quickly as possible. Its scope is less than that of the novel or novelette. However, it may deal with material which could also be presented in the form of a novel. In such a case, the special technique of the short-story lies in the selection of only those salient details of the material which will produce the desired unified effect as briefly as possible. It may vary in length from so brief a story as O. Henry's *The Gift of the Magi* to so lengthy a story as James's *The Turn of the Screw*.

The **novelette** (diminutive of "novel"), as the term implies, is a short novel. Its scope is larger than that of a short-story, and it is less compact. Generally it deals with fewer characters and incidents than the novel, is less complex, and presents a less extensive view of life. For example, Henry James's *Daisy Miller* and Edith Wharton's *Ethan Frome* may be classed as novelettes.

The **novel** is a long story which aims to produce a unified effect by embodying certain truths of experience in a series of imagined incidents or events. It is large in scope and often covers a number of diverse characters, scenes, and themes. Its plot tends to be highly complex. It may make use of many varieties of subject matter, and of any or all the devices of narrative technique, while its variations upon the purpose of fiction are as numerous as its authors. Some famous examples of the novel are Scott's *Ivanhoe*, Thackeray's *Henry Esmond*, Dickens's *A Tale of Two Cities*, Twain's *Huckleberry Finn*, Maugham's *Of Human Bondage*, and Lewis's *Babbitt*.

[A form originally a forerunner of the novel, and often associated with it, is the **romance**. Actually a romance is not a fictional form at all. It is, in general, merely a work of fiction, variable in length and scope, with strongly marked romantic characteristics. Its true distinguishing features are its subject material and its peculiar interests. Among these may be noted its interest in action and story, its exaggeration and idealization of character, its fondness for the adventuresome, the unusual, and the fabulous, and its emphasis upon the colorful, the picturesque, and the exotic. Malory's *Morte d'Arthur*, Spenser's *Faerie Queene*, Tennyson's *Idylls of the King* are romances, as are such varied products as M. G. Lewis's "Gothic romance," *The Monk*, the once-popular tales of H. Rider Haggard, Conan Doyle's *The Lost World*, and the interminable progeny of Edgar Rice Burroughs. In modern practice there is often little difference between the romance and the romantic novel.]

The mere size of a work of fiction is undoubtedly its most obvious manifestation of form. But if one examines further the matter of form, one will observe that form in fiction is principally determined by internal organization. This internal organization is governed by the necessity for producing an artistic **unity of effect.** But as the scope of fiction increases, the producing of a unified effect becomes more difficult, and necessitates the employment of more elaborate methods to unify its complexity.

The common means of achieving unity of effect in complex fiction are plot, character, setting, and theme. But such unity, it should be observed, is achieved, not merely as a result of emphasizing plot, character, or setting, but by using one or more as an agent in binding together the fabric of the whole composition. For example, in Defoe's *Robinson Crusoe* the emphasis is distinctly placed upon plot, but unity is achieved through the character of the protagonist. It is true, further, that in great works of fiction unity is frequently achieved by a joint use of plot, characters, setting, and theme. In most works of fiction, however, one method is commonly given precedence over the others.

The **unification of effect by means of plot** is perhaps the most obvious organization of material which produces form. As we have seen, there are two kinds of plot, the episodic and the organic. But the episodic plot, by its very nature, has a fluid development without real beginning or end, and consists of diverse episodes with little formal connection. The organic plot, on the contrary, is architectural in structure; its component parts are closely integrated to form a unified whole. As a consequence, the completed structure of an organic plot, like the bony framework of a skeleton, constitutes a definite design, and imposes a recognizable form upon the body of fiction. But it is obvious that such a unified form can be achieved only when the plot is organic.

The organic plot may achieve unity of effect in either of two ways. It may be so organized as to introduce first a situation, for which the subsequent story provides an explanation. This is the method of gaining unity in Wilkie Collins's *The Moonstone* and Kipling's *The Man Who Would Be King*. Or it may be so organized as to present actions and events which are seemingly unrelated, but which so converge upon each other as to maintain suspense until their merging demonstrates their essential correlation. This is the method of Scott's *Ivanhoe* and O. Henry's *The Gift of the Magi*.

The **unification of effect by means of character** gives form to several kinds of fiction. Thus, in its simplest application, the method may employ a single individual to unify and bind together the otherwise unrelated events of such episodic fiction as the picaresque story. The individual need not be a fully developed character, nor one carefully studied or individualized; he may merely participate in the various episodes of the story. It is largely thus that Defoe's *Robinson Crusoe* is given any semblance of unity.

In more complex fiction, particularly that which is biographical in effect, character becomes the center of organization. Here, as in Thackeray's *Henry Esmond* or Maugham's *Of Human Bondage,* the protagonist is presented in terms of those experiences which have modified and molded his personality, and it is this central personality which gives order and meaning to the details of the story. This method of unification results in what is known as the **biographical,** or **autobiographical, novel.**

Character is also frequently used as the means of unification in that highly complex type of modern fiction known as "stream of consciousness" fiction. Such fiction undertakes to set forth the relatively unselected details of action, plus the heterogeneous stream of mental impressions and concepts, which represent a brief segment of the life of an individual. Since the whole purpose is the revelation of the central figure in terms of all he is, physically, mentally, and emotionally, during a brief period of time—in James Joyce's *Ulysses,* only twenty-four hours—obviously it is this central character which unifies the whole organization of the story.

Although **unification of effect by means of setting** occurs rather infrequently, certain examples may be found. In these it is the setting which draws together the dispersed elements of the story and gives them the desired unity of effect. This use may be seen in Conrad's *Typhoon* and Norman Douglas's *South Wind.* In such a contemporary work as Vicki Baum's *Grand Hotel* it is the setting alone which gives any semblance of unity to what is, otherwise, almost a collection of separate episodes. More generally, however, setting is used as a secondary factor in support of plot, character, or theme. In Scott's *Ivanhoe,* the historical setting is used to support the unifying effect of plot; in Twain's *Huckleberry*

Finn, it is used to support character; in Dos Passos' *1919*
it is used to support theme.

The importance of the **unification of effect by means
of theme,** particularly in contemporary fiction, can hardly
be over-emphasized. Theme is, as we have seen, in its
simplest sense a part of the writer's philosophical interpretation of life. Its most obvious use as a means of
securing unity of effect in fiction is in stories which are
symbolized representations of the artist's abstract conceptions. In this sense it stands in relation to its fictional
embodiment much as the "moral" stands in relation to
one of Æsop's fables. For example, the theme of Hawthorne's *The Scarlet Letter* might be phrased, by a process
of over-simplification, as the homely aphorism "Murder
will out." More precisely, of course, the theme of that
novel is the various effects of evil as determined by the
circumstances governing individual characters.

But there are many kinds of fiction in which theme
serves as the unifying factor. There is **thesis** or **propa-
ganda fiction,** well illustrated by the work of H. G.
Wells and Upton Sinclair, in which the unifying theme
is a philosophical or social thesis, illustrated or proved by
the circumstances of the story. Then there is **problem
fiction,** in which the writer presents a situation in its entirety, and, without drawing conclusions, preaching ser-
mons, or pointing a moral, propounds an implicit question. It is largely the theme which unifies and gives form
to such problem novels as Ford's *A Man Could Stand Up*
and Dreiser's *An American Tragedy.* Furthermore, in
that kind of fiction to which the term "slice of life" has

been applied, particularly when the slice is taken length-wise, or through a period of time, theme is often the sole means of unifying the subject matter. Such stories, often referred to as the **saga type of fiction,** usually result in either an extremely long single novel or several novels grouped in a series. Their scope often includes the events of several generations with corresponding changes among the personnel of their characters. In such fiction it is the theme which holds together the various parts. Thus in Phyllis Bentley's *Inheritance* it is the introduction of machinery in nineteenth-century industry which serves as the unifying theme, and in Galsworthy's *Forsyte Saga* it is the growth and decay of a civilization.

In more recent developments in fiction, theme has taken on a somewhat altered meaning and has become even more important as a unifying force. By analogy, perhaps, with the use of the term in music, theme has come to mean an intellectual concept upon which the writer's impressions of life may be said to play variations. More specifically, the author presents a lateral cross-section of life, with breadth and depth, but with very little length in time, in which characters, setting, and plots may shift, vary, and blend with the anarchic irregu-larity of life itself. The author's impression of all this, backed, presumably, by a profound philosophic idea, serves as the theme of his work, and unifies the other-wise disconnected items into a coherent whole. This is the important function of theme in such impressionistic (or expressionistic—the two terms are loosely used almost interchangeably) novels as Aldous Huxley's *Point Coun-*

terpoint (the title of which, it will be noted, plays upon the notion of the theme in music) and John Dos Passos' *1919*. Thus the latter novel is a breadthwise cutting through the lives of many people in the post-war year of 1919. They have little or no connection with each other; they belong to no major plot; few of them proceed through the entire story, and none dominates the action. It is partly the setting of 1919 but more the author's impression of that year and its effects upon the lives of his characters which unifies the novel.

Form, then, in fiction may be considered the result of two factors: the scope of the work, and the organization of the material in such a way as to produce a unity of effect. That there may be no other factors one hesitates to say. For fiction is a type of literature in a constant state of flux. It is subject to constant experimentation. What the future may develop as an aid to form is not only perilous but impossible to predict.

CHAPTER V

THE TYPES OF LITERATURE: DRAMA

Drama differs from all other types of literary creation in that it is literature only in part. Indeed, one might speak of drama as really a fusion of the arts. Singly or altogether, it may, and often does, include a variety of kindred arts: music, painting, sculpture, architecture, pantomime, and the dance. For this reason the drama is a highly complex art, the discussion of which often leads to confusion.

It is well, therefore, to clarify at once certain basic matters respecting drama. In the most general sense, drama is simply the unified art of the theatre. But even in this general sense the term drama is ambiguous and needs further definition. At the risk of hair-line distinctions, let us try to clarify the problem.

Although the term *drama* has specific reference to a stage or theatrical presentation, through usage it has achieved a much wider meaning. We may speak, for example, of current events as full of drama; we may describe a painting, a bit of sculpture, a novel, or even an aspect of nature as dramatic, or containing drama. In this wider sense we are speaking of drama as something larger than literature, as an element in life and a component of all the arts.

If one examines further this dramatic property of life, one recognizes that its presence is usually identified by a sense of activity directed toward an issue. That is to say, one becomes aware of drama whenever activity of any sort ceases to imply an inevitable result and implies instead a decisive moment in which one of several possible conclusions is determined. This universal kind of drama results inevitably from conflict. The seasonal battles of the elements, the eternal warfare of man against nature, of man against man, and of man against himself, the clash of wills and personalities, the opposition of physical, mental and moral forces, result in drama whenever the combat reaches a moment of crisis. Since such a moment includes, of necessity, a sense of some outcome indeterminate but impending, it is bound to evoke in the observer some emotional response. It may be pity or terror, exaltation, pleasure, laughter or a sense of wonder. Thus a windstorm, a crisis in the wars of the elements, may cause in the observer either fear or exaltation; man's war against insect life has its moments of fear and wonder; man's battles against man, and against his own baser nature, his weakness, his cruelty, and his folly, will, at moments of crisis, produce mingled emotions: anger, pity, terror, disgust, pleasure, or laughter.

Drama, then, as a universal component of life and art, may be defined as any crisis, real or represented, resulting from conflict and productive of emotional intensity in the mind of an observer.

But universal drama, or the drama of life, as it might be called, has, of course, no technique of its own; its representation in any art is dependent upon the technique of the art form in which it is expressed. Consequently we can discuss it here only in its chief literary representation; that is, as it is embodied in the drama of the theatre, which has a specialized technique of its own. As for the representation of life's drama in other forms of literature, the technique employed is usually borrowed from or based upon the technique of the drama of the theatre.

This **drama of the theatre** may be defined as an interpretation of life through presentation before an audience of dramatic crises designed to evoke a specific emotional response by means of action and speech. Written drama— the drama which we read—is simply the scenario for the drama of the theatre, a scenario which must be given full expansion either by actual actors upon an actual stage or by imagined actors on the stage of the reader's mind.

Certain allied terms are also subject to confusion and therefore require careful differentiation. Thus for example, **the drama,** in contradistinction to *drama,* which has been explained above, is a term used to designate the artistic repository of the dramatic: in other words, plays in general, of a particular period or of all time. A **play** is a specific example of the drama. (Sometimes a play of serious and strongly emotional nature is spoken of as *a drama.*) A **theatre** or **playhouse** is a building designed for dramatic performances; but **the theatre** refers to the whole of theatrical activity regarded as a social institution. To illustrate: We are able to date with reasonable accuracy Shakespeare's *play, Henry VIII,* a good ex-

ample of the Elizabethan historical *drama,* by the fact
that it was referred to as a new play when in 1613 the
Globe *theatre* burned down during its presentation. This
is one of the few certain dates in the history of the Elizabethan *theatre.*

Drama, as we have seen, implies more than merely
theatrical art. Because of this fact, the effects produced
by dramatic technique may vary widely in character. In
an effort to distinguish the nature of these effects and
the mechanism used to produce them, certain terms are
commonly employed. The expression **good theatre,** for
example, means any artistic use of the resources of the
stage to produce successfully a desired effect upon an
audience. The term, it should be noted, is a general one
and always implies a tribute to the dramatist's artistry.
If the effect desired is appropriate to the circumstances
which produce it, and justly proportioned to them, both
the effect and the means of producing it are described as
genuinely **dramatic.** If, on the other hand, the theatrical
effect is an exaggeration of what is appropriate to the
circumstances, the effect and the method are characterized as **theatrical** or **stagey.**

I. Types of the Drama

Although the term "theatre" means specifically a certain kind of building, we have seen that it refers also to
an institution, irrespective of buildings, platforms, stages,
and machinery. The drama of the theatre can be presented
in the open air on a grassy slope, in a barn, a class room,
a church, or in any place where a company of people can

be gathered together to watch an actor or actors engaged in mimetic activity. Consequently, although the technique and conventions of the drama are often modified by the necessities of the playhouse for which a play is designed and by the form into which the dramatic story is to be cast, the type, or kind, of drama an artist chooses to write is independent of formal requirements.

The type of the drama is dependent upon two considerations. The first of these is the interest of the dramatist in developing either characters from whose nature a plot arises, or a plot to advance which characters are fabricated. The second consideration is the attitude of the dramatist toward the problems of life which result in dramatic crises. These he may look upon as serious and potentially tragic, recognizing that in appropriate circumstances their only solution is disaster. Or he may see them as readily soluble by the simple application of common sense and good humor, and therefore relatively unimportant in a reasonable scheme of things and even amusing and delightful. Or, finally, taking a middle ground, he may look upon the problems as serious enough but at the same time capable of solution by sensible adjustment of the elements involved. As a consequence, no problem appears as wholly tragic or wholly comic, but as a subtle blending of the two in which each is tempered by the other.

Character drama is a convenient designation for that kind of drama which is primarily concerned with the development of characters from whose nature a plot arises. In character drama the three possible attitudes of the dramatist toward his dramatic problem result in three corresponding types which are known respectively as tragedy, comedy, and serio-comedy, or serious drama. Although each of these constitutes a separate expression of dramatic art, not uncommonly they are found mingled in individual plays. With the exception, however, of serio-comedy, where such mingling is characteristic of the type, comic elements in tragedy and tragic elements in comedy are distinctly incidental and are usually colored by the dominant character of the type.

Tragedy is that type of drama which exhibits a character, or a group of characters, struggling vainly to avert a doom which is inevitable because it is the product of the protagonist's own nature and the circumstances in which he finds himself. To the problem of tragedy there can be no happy solution possible so long as the nature of the protagonist remains what it is, and his situation is one whose component elements he cannot alter. Consequently, all genuine tragedy has within it the quality of universality. That is, since tragedy is the inevitable issue of vulnerable human nature placed in a situation which betrays that vulnerability, the spectator is compelled to recognize two facts: first, that a similar tragic dilemma is potentially present in all human life; and, second, that the issue is determined by forces beyond human control. For this reason the observer can identify himself with the tragic protagonist and sympathize with him, feeling pity for his impotence and suffering, and terror before the relentless inevitability of his doom. It is this sympathetic identification and consciousness of inevitability, coupled with a recognition of man's dignity in adversity, and a sense of contact with final and infinite truth, which comprises the peculiar quality of tragedy. Such austere emotional heights are attained by but few dramatists, among whom may be mentioned Sophocles, in *Œdipus,* Shakespeare, in *Hamlet, Lear,* and *Macbeth,* Dryden, in *All for Love,* Ibsen, in *Pillars of Society,* and Galsworthy, in *Justice.*

Tragedies are variously classified according to the nature of the antagonist in the play. Thus *Œdipus* is usually called a **fate tragedy,** because fate seems to be the antagonist of Œdipus; *Lear* is often called a **personal flaw tragedy,** because the antagonist of the king seems to be an individual weakness within himself; while *Justice* is clearly a **tragedy of environment,** because all the forces which go to make up the environment of the protagonist are arrayed against him.

Comedy is that type of drama which exhibits characters temporarily involved in humorous or semi-serious complications and misadventures, who eventually solve their difficulties by the application of genial good sense, or see them disappear into thin air, as they should in a reasonably constituted world. Properly speaking, in true comedy there is no serious problem, since the dramatist's sense of proportion and spirit of mirth recognize no such problems in the situations of actual life. Consequently the deep emotions of the audience are neither involved nor aroused. Instead, as befits such a conception of life, the true mood of comedy is one of amused tolerance for human fallibilities and of amiable enjoyment of life's diverting complexities. Nevertheless, for all its lightness, wit, and laughter, comedy is no less effective than tragedy in casting light upon human character and in illuminating life with its flashes of universal truth. This universality is no small part of the distinction of such fine comedies as Shakespeare's *Twelfth Night* and *As You Like It,* Congreve's *The Way of the World,* Goldsmith's *She Stoops to Conquer,* and Maugham's *The Circle.*

In keeping with its prevailing spirit, comedy substitutes for strong emotional excitement a pleasurable sense of amusement and well-being or graceful sentiment. Its proper concerns are humor, wit, and satire (see p. 55). According to the distribution and relative emphasis of these elements, several varieties of comedy may be differentiated. **Pure comedy,** for instance, of the type of *Twelfth Night,* is so called because of its perfect incorporation of the pure spirit of comedy and its lack of any discordant serious or satirical element. Similarly, **romantic comedy,** such as *As You Like It,* exemplifies the pure comic spirit but adds the glamor of romance to set a pleasant emotional keynote for the play. Of that comedy which introduces satire, the most familiar kind is comedy of manners. **Comedy of manners**—*The Way of the World* or *The Circle*—receives its name from the fact that it is primarily concerned with the exhibition and satirical criticism of those manners and affectations which constitute the conventions of social intercourse. Since a social code usually requires a self-conscious, artificial organization of society, comedy of manners usually deals with the higher social orders and cultivates sophistication, smartness, and wit. A specialized variety of character comedy, popularized by Ben Jonson, is known as **comedy of humors.** This proceeds, by means of isolation in a series of caricatures, to throw into relief certain "humors," or dominant traits of human nature, for the purpose of critical study or satire. It may be found illustrated in such a play as Jonson's *Every Man in His Humour*.

In the middle ground, drama may involve problems serious enough for tragedy, but, because viewed as capable of happy solution, susceptible to partially comic interpretation. By contrary approach, the incongruities of comedy may be recognized as sufficiently important to be given serious implication. When this occurs the drama ceases to be purely comic and becomes satiric or semi-serious. This intermediate type of drama, neither tragedy nor comedy but partaking of the nature of both, has been variously termed serio-comedy, *drame,* comedy-drama, problem play, thesis drama, and tragi-comedy. **Serio-comic drama** may be briefly defined as that type of drama which, by sensible adjustment of situation or characters or both, shows characters proceeding through serious situations to a successful solution. Often universal in its scope, serio-comic drama is ordinarily concerned with domestic, social, and moral problems, to which it offers, usually, reasoned and plausible solutions. It is the satisfactory solution of the central problem, it should be noted, which is provided. Whether the characters have sufficient wisdom to adapt themselves to the solution and arrive thereby at a happy dénouement, or the reverse, is another matter and may vary among plays. Thus one must not expect that the dénouement of serio-comedy will always coincide with what is known as a "happy ending." So problems of life are solved, not always to the final happiness of the characters involved, by Shakespeare in *The Tempest,* by Ibsen in *A Doll's House,* and by Barrie in *Dear Brutus.*

Serio-comic drama is difficult to classify because it is susceptible to almost infinite variations in the nature of the problem dramatized, and in the relatively serious or comic treatment of that problem. A few important varieties, however, have been given specific names. The term **problem play,** usually modified by such an adjective as domestic, social, political, etc., refers to any serio-comic drama which revolves about a problem described by the modifying adjective. For example, Ibsen's *A Doll's House* is called a **domestic problem play** because its core is a problem of family life.

The term **tragi-comedy,** similarly, is applicable to at least two types of plays: one which places the characters in great danger only to save them, logically, however, at the last; and one which is composed of two separate threads of action, one serious, the other comic. Shakespeare's *The Merchant of Venice* is an example of the former type. *Much Ado About Nothing* may be taken as an example of the latter type, the plot of Claudio and Hero forming the serious action and the plot of Beatrice and Benedick forming the comic action.

A **satiric drama** is a serious play in which the ridicule is so colored by moral earnestness that the play moves more to contempt or perturbation than to amiable laughter. Of this satiric drama, Shakespeare's *Measure for Measure* and Jonson's *Volpone* exemplify the more bitter aspect, while lighter and more laughable illustrations may be found today in the plays of Bernard Shaw.

So-called **sentimental drama** (or sentimental comedy) is simply a problem drama solved through the mediation of sentiment instead of logic, as in perhaps its best example, Steele's *The Conscious Lover,* or, a more modern example, Channing Pollock's *The Fool.*

So far we have been concerned with drama which is dominated by character. In drama, on the other hand, wherein plot is primary and characters are largely manufactured to fit its specifications, the dramatist's attitude toward the problems of life is manifestly of little consequence. Where the dramatist's volition is the sole arbiter of plot, obviously inevitability vanishes. The most one can expect is enough logic in the motivation to make the course of events seem reasonably plausible. Such problems as are presented are of the dramatist's own making and are solved according to his caprice. Actual life has very little to do with it. For this reason it is vain to look in plot drama for universality of application or serious philosophy of life. Its virtues are the incidental virtues of rapid action, effective scene, and momentary highlight. As a consequence, plot drama is generally considered an order of theatrical art inferior to drama of character.

Of **plot drama** there are three common varieties. These are known respectively as melodrama, farce, and intrigue comedy.

Melodrama is a term rather loosely, and somewhat incorrectly, used to designate the more serious varieties of plot drama. Originally it referred to a kind of music drama with the usual artifices and exaggerations of the type. By extension, it means any serious plot drama dominated by either chance or intrigue, in which are emphasized incident and action, sensational theatrical effects, and exaggerated emotions. Ordinarily melodrama presents puppet-like characters who are manipulated into unfortunate or dangerous situations and rescued therefrom by an often illogical chance or character reversal. As a rule, melodrama has a fortunate ending; nevertheless it must be recognized that such a play as *Romeo and Juliet,* with its factitious suspense and sensationalism, and its incidents independent of character, is definitely melodramatic for all its tragic dénouement. While melodrama is rarely great drama, it is often excellent theatre and sound art, as in Shakespeare's play just named, or in Boucicault's *The Octoroon,* Gillette's *Secret Service,* Capek's *R.U.R.,* and the legion of mystery and crime melodramas represented by such a notable example as Rinehart and Hopwood's *The Bat.*

In the comic realm, plot drama resolves itself inevitably into comedy of situation. That is, the comedy arises from the absurdity of the situations in which characters find themselves. The two chief varieties of this comedy of situation are farce and intrigue comedy.

Farce is the simplest form of comedy of situation. It depends upon broad incongruities, often the result of fatuous blundering or misapprehension. Its favorite devices are the obvious use of broad innuendo, horseplay and slapstick. Since its primary concern is the absurdity of the situation irrespective of its plausibility, it tends toward exaggeration beyond all bounds of probability. Rarely, if ever, it employs wit, satire, or the humorous exploitation of character. Although it may appear un-diluted in an entire play, more often it combines or alternates with higher elements of comedy. Thus Shakespeare's *Comedy of Errors* is nearly pure farce; Sheridan's *The Rivals* mingles farce with higher comedy; and Brandon Thomas's *Charley's Aunt* is pure farce.

Intrigue comedy is related to farce inasmuch as it, too, is comedy of situation. It differs from farce in its lack of rough incident and horseplay. Intrigue comedy is that type of play which arouses laughter by means of a series of delicately conceived and executed situations leading to innumerable mistakes and an amusing dénouement. Since these situations do not arise naturally from the characters, they are usually the result of deliberate trickery and scheming engaged in by one or more characters in the play. It is this motivation of the plot by intrigue which gives to the type its name. Often it shades into farce so closely that the two types are almost indistinguishable. Shakespeare's *Taming of the Shrew* and *The Merry Wives of Windsor,* for example, may be called either farces or comedies of intrigue, according to one's critical taste. The comedies of Fletcher and Dryden, however, notably *The Wild Goose Chase* of the former, and *An Evening's Love* of the latter, are distinctly intrigue comedies.

II. Elements of the Drama

Drama, as a literary art, has been described as the presentation before an audience of crises arising from conflict and issuing in a dénouement. Since this presentation amounts to a telling of the story of such crises, it will be seen that drama is really a kind of narrative. For this reason drama and fiction have a great deal in common. Although they vary widely in their selection of materials and methods of presentation, they are closely akin in their component elements.

For both deal with human themes and subjects, real, imaginary, or symbolized. Both present an event or series of events so organized and interpreted as to present a meaningful illusion of reality. Both have plots, characters, settings, themes, tempos, and points of view. However, the methods of selecting and presenting these materials may differ because of their divergent purposes and media of expression.

As we have seen, the purpose of the dramatist is to convey his interpretation of life to an audience composed of many people seated in a theatre. The purpose of the writer of fiction, on the other hand, is to convey his interpretation to a single reader. Obviously, the necessity of producing a single unified impression upon an audience composed of diverse minds and personalities imposes a heavy burden upon the dramatist. Furthermore, his time is limited. Into the brief compass of two or three hours' action, while maintaining the utmost of clarity and emotional force, he must concentrate all his material.

But the audience is only one of the factors determining the technique of the dramatist. His medium of expression, the theatre, is even more important. In this land of make-believe, the purely physical restrictions of the stage have necessitated a number of conventions, matters which audience and playwright have tacitly agreed to accept without question. The stage itself, a three-sided room with one wall mysteriously missing, is a convention, as are such matters as the raisings and lowerings of the curtain, the arbitrary movements of actors, the shifts in time and place, and the selective concentration of action. As a consequence, the successful dramatist must be not only a creative artist but also a man of the theatre, a master of his medium of expression.

Like fiction, drama is composed primarily of three elements: characters, plot, and setting. Since the nature and use of these is practically the same in drama and fiction, and the methods of their development and artistic treatment nearly identical, there is no need for repeating here the discussion already devoted to them. (See pp. 82-92.) It will be enough to relate them to drama and point out such modifications as the dramatic medium makes advisable.

Thus drama may present a **typical character,** such as Orlando in Shakespeare's *As You Like It,* or Maurya in Synge's *Riders to the Sea;* or an **individual character,** such as Falstaff in *Henry IV,* Lady Kitty in Maugham's *The Circle,* or Brutus Jones in O'Neill's *The Emperor Jones.* For purposes of satirical comedy it may employ a **caricature** (or "humorous character," as Ben Jonson called it) like Pistol in *Henry IV*, Bobadill in Jonson's *Every Man in His Humour*, and Sir Benjamin Backbite in Sheridan's *School for Scandal*, or Mrs. Malaprop in *The Rivals*. These characters, like those of fiction, may change and develop or remain static. The **developing characters** are usually the central figures of a play. Such characters are Shakespeare's Macbeth, O'Neill's Brutus Jones, and Nora in Ibsen's *A Doll's House*. **Static characters,** on the other hand, are usually minor figures, like the whole cast of *Romeo and Juliet* except for the two lovers.

One kind of character used a great deal in drama is known as the **stock character.** A stock character is any character which by frequent association with a particular kind of play or dramatic situation has come to be looked upon as a conventional adjunct of such a play or situation. Stock characters are the cogs required for the smooth operation of certain kinds of dramatic machinery. For instance, the persecuted heroine and the sleek villain are stock figures of cheap melodrama, as are the preoccupied husband, the lonely wife, and the "other man" in so-called "triangle" plays. Such characters may be either typical or individualized. Both Oliver in *As You Like It* and Iago in *Othello* are stock villains; but Oliver is a typical villain while Iago is realized as an individual.

In his methods of **character exposition** the dramatist is greatly restricted by his medium. Obviously he is unable to describe, analyze, or comment upon his characters except through the mouths of other characters in the play.

Thus the implicit method of characterization (see p. 88) is the only one open to him.

The **dramatic function** of characters is similar to the function of characters in fiction. Thus Nora, in *A Doll's House,* and O'Neill's Emperor Jones have the function of **protagonist.** (The terms "hero" and "heroine" should be applied to the protagonist only when he or she is truly heroic in the full sense of the word.) The **antagonist** may be an individual, such as Shylock in *The Merchant of Venice;* or fate, as in *Romeo and Juliet* or the *Œdipus* of Sophocles; or environment, as in Galsworthy's *Justice;* or some inner force, weakness, evil, or ambition, as in *Macbeth* and *King Lear.* Often, of course, the antagonist in drama is a combination of many forces both internal and external.

Among minor characters, the **foil** may be illustrated in *Hamlet* by Laertes, who serves in that capacity to the prince; or in *Henry IV* by Hotspur, who is both foil and antagonist to Prince Hal. The **confidant** is of prime value in drama since he affords a listener to more important characters and thus provides a most necessary opportunity for exposition of character and plot. To this end, Horatio is the confidant of Hamlet, and Mrs. Linden of Nora in *A Doll's House.* Mere **background characters** are used sparingly in drama, for its strict economy forbids the squandering of precious time upon characters who do not materially advance its action. Only in plays which stress and personify ideas and social types, such as Toller's *Masses and Men* and Gorki's *The Lower Depths,* are characters of value as background, and then they often are not even named. For the character as **narrator** there is obviously no place in the drama. What resembles an extension of the function, however, sometimes appears in plays which hinge upon a problem or thesis. This character, who seems to speak for the dramatist, and who discusses and points the theme, is known as the **raisonneur,** and may be illustrated by Candida in Shaw's *Candida* or by an early example, Friar Laurence in *Romeo and Juliet*.

The plot of drama, like that of fiction, may be either episodic or organic. The **episodic** plot, which in drama is the less common form, may be seen in such plays as *Romeo and Juliet* and Drinkwater's *Abraham Lincoln*. The **organic plot** may be illustrated by *Hamlet, A Doll's House*, or indeed by almost any modern drama. Its structural elements are those of fiction: exposition, involution (rising action), climax, and resolution (falling action and dénouement). In only two is there any appreciable difference. **Dramatic exposition** can be given to the audience only in terms of dialogue and action. It therefore becomes an important matter of dramatic technique to introduce the exposition within these limitations in as natural and inconspicuous a manner as possible. Inept or arbitrary methods are often described as mechanical exposition. The **dramatic climax,** like that of fiction, is the moment, coming usually near the end of a play, when the conflicting forces are brought into decisive opposition. Since the circumstances of dramatic presentation demand a clear-cut issue, such decisive opposition is quite explicit, and the scene in which it occurs is often referred to as **"the obligatory scene."** But, besides this climax in the physical action, there often occurs in the drama a moment in which both the emotional tone of the play and the emotional reaction of the audience are brought to a peak of intensity. This emotional high point is known as the **emotional climax.** It may or may not coincide with the physical climax. In *Hamlet,* for example, whereas the dramatic climax is reached toward the end of the play, the emotional climax is reached in the third act, in Hamlet's interview with his mother.

Although, in general, the dramatist is limited to action and dialogue for the development of his play, he is permitted to use as aids to that development certain specialized dramatic devices. These devices are often highly unnatural, but since their use is accepted as a part of the general convention of the stage, they do not destroy the dramatic illusion. Frequently of value in the development of characters, setting, and theme, their main use is as an aid to the conduct of the plot. Of such nature are the following.

Stage business, as indicated in the stage directions in the written version of the play, is the total amount of action in the play. Stage business deals with entrances, exits, movements upon the stage, and the pantomimic expression of emotion.

Entrances and **exits** are determined by three principles: (1) that the stage should be rarely, if ever, left vacant, (2) that no character should be left alone upon the stage (unless for the purpose of soliloquy or pantomime), and (3) that a character should move on and off the stage in as natural a manner as possible when his presence or absence is required by the action. Entrances and exits are used to arrange the fluent merging of one scene or situation with another. In older drama this use was recognized by the definite indication of scenes, the entrance or departure of a character being marked by a scene division.

Movements upon the stage are either upstage (that is, toward the rear of the stage), downstage (toward the footlights), or left or right (that is, according to the left or right of the actor as he faces the audience). Such movements are conventionally conditioned by the necessity, first, of maintaining a symmetrical grouping and balancing of the stage picture and, second, of enabling the audience to see what is going on. Movements are used to work out the physical action of the plot and to maintain the visual attention of the audience.

Pantomime, the interpretation of emotion or thought through gestures and facial expressions, is an invaluable aid to characterization as well as to the conduct of the plot. It is used to supplement and enforce dialogue, and its effectiveness is limited only by the imagination of the writer and the skill of the actor.

Exposition of the plot and general situation can be given by both dialogue and action. In addition, several specialized devices are often used. **Letters, telegrams,** and **notes,** are usually read aloud upon the stage, so that their contents may be revealed to the audience. The **so-**

liloquy, or dramatic monologue (see p. 23), the **aside** (a brief speech made to the audience while other characters on the stage affect not to hear), and the **stage whisper** (a speech "whispered" at the top of the speaker's lung power) are other unnatural but effective means of conveying necessary information to the audience. Although the soliloquy and the aside are usually found only in older drama, their use in modern drama is effectively demonstrated in O'Neill's *Strange Interlude.*

Other devices useful to the conduct of the plot are foreshadowing, repetition and contrast, peripetia, dramatic irony, *deus ex machina,* and poetic justice. Each of these has a distinct dramatic value.

Foreshadowing is a hint or suggestion to the audience of the probable outcome of a course of action. It arouses the expectations of the audience, increases its feeling of suspense and, at the same time, enables the dramatist to point up the significance of a specific passage. See, for example, Juliet's farewell speech to Romeo:

> O God! I have an ill-divining soul:
> Methinks I see thee, now thou art so low,
> As one dead in the bottom of a tomb:
> Either my eyesight fails, or thou look'st pale.
> (*Romeo and Juliet,* III, v)

Repetition and contrast are effective means of emphasizing and clarifying situations and characters. **Repetition** (or **parallelism**) is the use more than once of substantially the same plot, character, speech, sentiment, or situation in the same play. Thus the main plot of Lear and his daughters, in *King Lear,* is repeated in, or paralleled by, the sub-plot of Gloucester and his sons. In Dryden's alteration of Shakespeare's *The Tempest,* the younger dramatist added to the cast the character of a boy who had never seen a woman, parallel to Miranda who had never seen a man. **Contrast,** on the other hand, is the opposition of characters or scenes. It may be represented by an alternation of light and serious episodes or scenes, each by contrast enhancing the other; or it may be represented by such an opposition as the contrast of Cordelia's goodness with the evil of her sisters, in *King Lear.*

Peripetia, a device which heightens the dramatic intensity of a scene, is a rapid and complete reversal in the fortunes of a character. It may be represented by a sudden fall, as when Romeo, happy in his recent marriage, is forced into a duel with Tybalt, with fatal consequences, or by a sudden rise, as when Viola, in *Twelfth Night,* about to be led to her death, is recognized as a woman and offered marriage by Orsino. In the latter form it is often used to produce the dénouement of comedy.

Dramatic irony is a slightly modified form of irony proper (see p. 54). It is a mechanical device whereby in any situation a character is made to anticipate an outcome which the audience knows will be realized, but with consequences contrary to those anticipated. In effect, it is an anticipated peripetia. The emotional response of the audience is heightened by its exclusive perception of the irony. Thus in Shakespeare's *Richard III,* Hastings, unaware of the tragic situation prepared for him by Richard, speaks of the duke thus:

> His grace looks cheerfully and smooth to-day;
> There's some conceit or other likes him well,
> When that he bids good morrow with such spirit.
> I think there's never a man in Christendom
> Can lesser hide his love or hate than he;
> For by his face straight you shall know his heart.
>   (*Richard III*, III, iv)

The conceit which so pleased the duke, as the audience knows, is his plot for getting rid of the hopeful Hastings, and a moment later that worthy is accused of witchcraft and condemned to his death.

Deus ex machina is a term borrowed from Greek drama where it applied to the use of a god (an actor brought on the stage in a "machine") to change arbitrarily the course of an action. In its later use it means any force in the play which has absolute power to determine the course of an action. Thus Oberon in *A Midsummer Night's Dream* arbitrarily alters the course of things to suit himself, as does Prospero in *The Tempest*.

Since it is the purpose of drama to produce a sustained and unified impression, it is necessary for the dénouement to create an illusion of rounded completeness in the action and theme. In the interests of economy and sharply defined clarity, this often involves the use of conventional and artificial devices. Among them is the observance of what is called poetic justice. **Poetic justice** is a just apportionment of rewards and punishments for the actions in a play in accordance, not with normal probability, but with the logic of art, which insists that there be left no loose ends and that the essence of perfection is proportion and the harmonious adjustment of part to part. Thus poetic justice demands that an action be completed by a fitting recompense, as, in *The Merchant of Venice,* Shylock is fittingly punished for his attempt on Antonio's life. An extended form of poetic justice, commonly known as **Hebrew justice,** applies the principle of an "eye for an eye" and demands that recompense be meted out in kind as well as degree.

As for the **tempo** of a play, ordinarily it must be made to appear that of normal life. Since the illusion of drama is one of eavesdropping upon a series of actual occurrences, obviously a large part of the illusion depends upon a tempo which corresponds to that of real life. Nevertheless, the high selectivity and condensation of the plot tend to compress the action, so that the tempo of drama is actually faster than that of normal life. Delays, pauses, and the intervals between actions are eliminated. As a result, the actual tempo is accelerated, and the *real time,* that is, the time occupied by the actual production of the play, is usually less than the *ideal time,* that is, the time which the events shown *seem* to cover.

This telescoping of time may be achieved by various methods. The dropping of the curtain and its immediate raising is often used to indicate the lapse of an hour or two of ideal time. Characters may leave the stage for a stated interval, and return in much less time than the period stated, the attention of the audience being distracted, meanwhile, by further action on the stage. Similarly, off-stage actions, journeys, and the like, which would normally consume considerable ideal time, are often accomplished in incredibly brief periods of real time, the brevity of which, however, the audience usually accepts without question. In addition, the nature of the drama and its emotional tone tend to influence tempo. Thus the discussion of ideas moves more slowly than witty repartee; a deeply emotional scene requires more time than the antics of farce; comedy moves more rapidly than tragedy.

The **setting** of drama differs from that of fiction in that ordinarily it is presented to the actual view of the audience instead of being merely described. Nevertheless, in certain kinds of drama, like that of Shakespeare, designed for an unfurnished or simply appointed stage, the setting may be suggested or described by the characters and embellished by the imagination of the audience. In some experimental plays, particularly those which use impressionistic or expressionistic settings, the setting is no more than suggested or symbolized. Such is the case in Rice's *The Adding Machine* and Kaufman and Connelly's *Beggar on Horseback,* although such production methods may be applied to a wide variety of plays.

III. FORMS OF THE DRAMA

As we have seen, drama in the theatre is a presentation of a crisis in human affairs resulting in a dénouement. The available media for such a presentation are action, speech and music. According to the combination of these, and the relative emphasis devoted to each, different varieties of theatrical presentation result. Thus a dramatic presentation which involves action alone is called

pantomime. Action coupled with music results in a **dance** or **ballet.** The harmonious fusion of action, speech and music is known as **opera.** When speech and action are combined and music used only incidentally or not at all, the result is **a play.**

Now the important fact to recognize about these variant forms of expression is that they all constitute drama. Substantially, in purpose, form and structure, they are one and the same. It is in scope that they are bound to vary. There is a limit to what can be conveyed to an audience by action or music alone, or by a combination of the two. Even in the two most elaborate and inclusive forms, the play and the opera, there is a difference in resources and opportunity. By its very nature, a play is better adapted to the treatment of ideas and the subtleties of character revelation, while the opera excels in the creation of a mood and the enforcement of emotional values. Between the opera and the play lie several hybrid varieties which combine the characteristics of both in varying degrees. The most common of these are the **comic opera,** the **operetta,** the **musical comedy,** and the **play with music.** Although each of these has its own peculiar qualities, conventions, and specialized technique, they lie beyond the scope of this book and need not be discussed.

For, although structurally they are all much the same, we are here concerned primarily with drama as literature. As a type of literature, closely related to fiction, its form, much like that of fiction, is largely determined by its scope and by the structural organization necessary to achieve unity of effect. Since, however, these general factors have been discussed in connection with fiction (see pp. 100 and 104), it is important here to discuss only the specific formal structure of that combination of speech and action called a play.

A play is a specific example of the drama. In its full length form it requires from two to three hours for its representation on the stage. Usually a play is made up of a number of structural divisions. These are act, scene, prologue, and epilogue.

An **act** is a division of a full length play which marks the stages of organic or episodic development of the action. The division of a play into acts corresponds roughly to the division of a novel into sections or chapters. The act division is also useful in a play as indicating the lapse of long periods of time: weeks, months or years. Practically, on the modern stage, the interval between acts is useful to permit the setting of the stage for a different scene and to permit the actors to change costumes and catch their breath. For the audience the act division is useful as a period of rest between longer periods of concentration. In modern practice most dramatists strive for a "good curtain" at the end of each act: that is, a minor climax which will carry over the suspense of the audience to the next act. Most modern full length plays are divided into three acts. Older drama was usually in five acts. Some few plays, such as Shaw's *Getting Married,* employ no formal act or scene divisions. Others, for example, O'Neill's *The Emperor Jones,* are divided into scenes only.

A **scene** is a formal subdivision of an act or of a whole

play used to mark a shift in action or in time and place. In older drama, with its accretive structure and simple settings, numerous formal scene divisions were used. In modern drama scenes are usually merged into one another within the structure of the act, and the formal scene division is used only to indicate a shift in time or place.

The **prologue** and the **epilogue** are, primarily, short spoken addresses to the audience, the first preceding the play, the second following it. The prologue is customarily used as a simple introduction to the play, while the epilogue may comment on the play and take a graceful leave of the audience. The prologue and epilogue to Drinkwater's *Abraham Lincoln* are typical. By extension, any division of the play which precedes the first act is called a prologue, and any division which follows the last act is called an epilogue. An example of the expanded prologue, which provides, in effect, an exposition of the central idea of the play, is the prologue to Rachel Crothers's *Mary the Third*. The expanded epilogue, which provides information additional to that conveyed in the completed play, is exemplified by the epilogue to Capek's *R.U.R.*, or that to Shaw's *St. Joan.*

Properly speaking, there is really but one completely developed form of drama, the play. But within itself the play may vary in accordance with two quite different structural patterns. These two structural patterns may be designated as the unfolding structure and the accretive structure. Both are found in drama of the present day, although the former is far more common than the latter. The first owes its origin to the classic drama of ancient

Greece; the second derives largely from the romantic drama of the sixteenth and seventeenth centuries.

The **unfolding structure** is that of a play which exposes or develops a dramatic situation by a process of revelation. Nearly all the elements of the situation are present at the beginning of the play, but they are only gradually revealed to the audience. Such a play seems to have little movement in time or space, the whole action often requiring only a few hours of ideal time, and frequently only one scene for its development. In the unfolding structure the emphasis is laid upon the reactions of characters to the situation.

The classic example of the unfolding structure is the Greek tragedy. In this form of drama, since the story to be told was one already familiar to the audience, the dramatist could confine himself to a presentation of only the result of a series of actions which had taken place before the play opened. Consequently Greek tragedy emphasized the gradual revelation of the situation and the effect thereof upon the characters involved. Its structure, therefore, was closely knit and highly unified. It began with a prologue or introduction, which briefly recapitulated the preceding action and general circumstances of the situation. Then followed five episodes, separated by intervening choral odes, each of which represented a new phase of the total revelation. The conclusion, or exode, summed up the significance of the complete revelation and pointed its meaning. Through a process of gradual modification this has come to be the most common form of contemporary drama. It may be found illustrated in such diverse plays as Sophocles's *Œdipus,* Ibsen's *Ghosts,* Shaw's *Candida,* and O'Neill's *Mourning Becomes Electra.*

A further characteristic of the Greek drama, and of its modern structural descendants, is its adherence to the Aristotelian unities of action, time and place. Because of the nature of its theatre and its material Greek drama was presented as a single unified action (that is, as only one thread of plot, with no sub-plot, extraneous characters, or incidental situations), taking place in one scene and within the compass of not more than twenty-four hours of ideal time. These observations of Aristotle became in later centuries rules for the conduct of drama, and they formed a difficult subject of contention in the sixteenth and seventeenth centuries, and even later. Obviously, adherence to such rules is impossible for any other than the unfolding form of drama, but it is noteworthy that in much of modern drama, no doubt without specific reference to the so-called law of the unities, there is a strong tendency toward the maintenance of a single action, in a single place, working toward its dénouement within the period of a few hours of ideal time. Bernard Shaw claimed this distinction for his play, *Getting Married,* and numerous other examples might be cited.

The **accretive structure** is that of a play which builds up a dramatic situation by a progressive addition of new characters, facts, and episodes. Originally there is no dramatic situation presented; as the play proceeds, moving in ideal time and space, it acquires a constantly increasing dramatic effect resulting from the complications of the newly added material. The emphasis in the accretive structure is laid upon those actions of the characters which result from their reactions to situations.

The common example of the accretive structure is the romantic play of the Elizabethan age. But this, in turn, resulted from more primitive forms, the **miracle** and the **morality,** with a borrowing of the five act division from classic drama. These forms, although primitive and largely replaced by later modifications, have maintained something of an independent existence down to modern times. For example, Max Reinhardt's *The Miracle,* first presented in New York in 1924, and the Passion Plays presented in Oberammergau, Germany, are modern miracle plays, while *Everyman,* an early example of a morality play, is still occasionally produced in the modern theatre. The loosest example of the accretive structure, the **pageant,** a presentation of scenes and characters representing or symbolizing an event or an idea, takes its name from the wagon on which the original miracle plays were performed. The pageant is still popular, as may be seen in the various historical pageants presented in the United States in connection with specific holidays or festivals.

The structure of all such naïve drama, since it told a simple story, was consequently accretive. Romantic drama took over and crystallized this accretive structure, and it has remained much the same to the present day. Examples of the accretive structure include Shakespeare's *Othello,* and *Cymbeline,* Rostand's *Cyrano de Bergerac,* and Shaw's *St. Joan.*

In addition to the play proper two other shorter forms

of the drama are to be noted, the one-act play, and the dramatic skit, or sketch. As the play is comparable to the novel of fiction, so the one-act play is comparable to the short-story, and the skit to the anecdote, or the short short-story. The **one-act play** is a short play with a single, highly unified and compressed structure, few characters, and developed with the utmost economy of means to produce a single dramatic effect. The **skit,** or **sketch,** is simply a bit of dramatic dialogue which springs a "nub," or point, in short order. Originally related to the mediæval *interlude,* which it resembles, its use on the modern stage is largely in the revue or in vaudeville.

A specialized form of short play, chiefly of historical importance, is the masque. The **masque** is a poetic drama, with full accompaniments of music and dance, designed to be produced by amateur actors on very elaborate stages. It is usually found in three parts: the *entry,* or the first movements of the masquers in dancing processional, the *main,* or body of the production, which consists of poetic speeches, songs and spectacular scenic effects, and the *going out,* or exit dance. Highly romantic in tone, it is frequently distinguished by the presence of pastoralism, classical allusion, mythology, magic, and allegory. The masques of Ben Jonson and Milton's *Comus* are famous examples.

CHAPTER VI

THE TYPES OF LITERATURE: POETRY

Any attempt to explain the exact nature of poetry is beset by the initial difficulty that there does not exist, and never has existed, any very definite and generally accepted understanding of what poetry specifically is. Many poets and critics have essayed definitions of poetry, but without entire success. The difficulty may be inferred from the two characteristics of poetry noted by the poet Edwin Arlington Robinson: "One is that it is, after all, undefinable. The other is that it is eventually unmistakable."

For poetry is a matter of both content and form. Traditionally and conventionally its form of expression is verse, in contradistinction to prose. But poetry is at times found expressed in a prose medium, and mere use of verse does not make poetry. Obviously, then, poetry implies more than mere verse form.

Originally the word poetry seems to have meant simply artistic creation. In this sense it would apply to the whole realm of creative and imaginative literature. Its opposite, as Coleridge pointed out, would thus be not prose but science. During the passage of time, however, poetry has become more restricted in scope, has acquired certain delimiting qualities, and has evolved a specialized technique adapted to the achievement of its peculiar ends. Since it is this technique—this means whereby poetry attains artistic expression—which is our principal concern, it is therefore more practical to abandon the vexed problem of what poetry ultimately is, and restrict ourselves to certain recognizable aims of poetry and the mechanical means whereby they are accomplished.

The peculiar quality of poetry can be distinguished from that of prose if one thinks of the creative mind as normally expressing itself in a variety of literary forms ranged along a graduated scale between the two contrasted extremes of scientific exposition and lyrical verse. Along this scale the literary forms differ not so much in kind as in degree. Midway one finds such intermediary forms as rhapsodical prose, prose poems, free verse, and some oratory, in which the attitude, content, and technique of prose and poetry are so intermingled that it is difficult to say whether the effect is that of one or of the other.

By considering lyrical poetry, or song, as an extreme example of poetic qualities, it is possible to observe those characteristics which all poetry possesses to a greater or less degree. In particular, one may note that (1) there is a use of rhythmic and musical effects to enhance the meaning of language; (2) there is an effort to create vivid impressions by directly stimulating the senses; (3) there is an intensity of emotional appeal; and (4) the language is especially choice, selective, and connotative. These, of course, are the rudiments of all artistic expression, not only of poetry. But it is in the distinctive combination and adaptation of them that poetry captures that quintessential magic which is the soul of its being.

The primary purpose of poetry, as of all art, is to afford pleasure through the contemplation of beauty—in thought, feeling, expression and technical skill. But in so doing, its intent is to transmit an experience in its entirety: not only the physical details, but also their total meaning, the emotional reactions aroused, and the mental reflections stimulated by the experience. Moreover, poetry endeavors to induce sensuously a mood appropriate to the content of the poem. It strives for a conviction begotten of the emotions rather than of the reason. It tries to put the reader into a state of awareness wherein the truth and beauty of its subject will appear as self-evident and indisputable.

The approach of poetry is indirect. It proceeds by means of suggestion, implication, reflection. Its method is largely symbolical. It is more interested in connotations than in denotations. Its language is determined quite as much by its suggestive properties as by its exact meaning. The peculiar feature of poetry is that, by a combination of its technical devices, it constantly endeavors to suggest more than can adequately be put into words.

I. Prosody

To accomplish its purposes poetry, of course, may utilize all the mechanical devices of imagery, association, and sound which are common to literature. Perhaps the most obvious, however, of its characteristics is its musical quality, or, in more general terms, the use which it makes of sound to reënforce sense or to give pleasure for its own sake. For this reason poetry achieves its complete effect only when read aloud or with the inner ear keenly attuned to sound values.

The sound values of poetry are of two general kinds: (1) those which fall under the classification of rhythm, and (2) those under the classification of tone color. Each of these values is considered fully below.

Rhythm, as a general literary phenomenon, has already been discussed (p. 42 ff.). It is common to both poetry and prose. A specialized form of rhythm, however, has for centuries been conventionally associated with poetry. This form is known as verse.

Verse is rhythm which is arranged according to a regular and uniform pattern.

[The word "verse," used in a different sense, also means a line of poetry. "Verse" is used incorrectly as an equivalent for the word "stanza."]

This regular time and stress pattern of verse is called **meter.** The metrical analysis of verse for purposes of study is known as **scansion. Prosody,** or **versification,** is the term applied to the technique of verse, particularly as it is concerned with meter.

Meter, of course, means "measure." In versification it refers specifically to the measuring of the number and kinds of units which constitute a line of verse. The unit of measurement in verse is called a foot or measure. A **verse foot** is an invariable time interval between two regular beats or stresses in the verse rhythm. The following lines may be divided into feet thus:

I aríse | from dréams | of theé
In the fírst | sweet sleép | of níght,
When the wínds | are breáth|ing lów,
And the stárs | are shín|ing bríght.
            (Shelley: *Indian Serenade*)

Two characteristics of the foot should be noted: (1) each foot is marked by a metrical beat, and (2) the time interval between beats remains roughly constant.

Meter is built upon three inherent properties of speech: stress or accent, the lapse of time necessary for the articulation of sounds, and the natural rhythmic movement imparted by meaning to phraseology. Each of these affects the character of the foot, while the combination of all three produces the various kinds of feet recognizable in English verse.

For practical purposes in reading English verse, it is the regular recurrence of beats which marks off the feet of the meter. Since in general these beats coincide with the accented syllables of the words, it is relatively simple to divide a line into its component units. For the sake of convenience, lines of verse are described, as to the number of feet which they contain, by a series of terms compounded of the Greek numerals and the word meter (i.e., measure). These terms are **monometer, dimeter, trimeter, tetrameter, pentameter, hexameter, heptameter, octameter, nonameter;** and refer respectively to metrical lines containing from one to nine feet.

Examples of the first five kinds of meter are contained in the following stanza from Herrick's ode to Ben Jonson:

> Ah Ben!   (1)
> Say how, or when   (2)
> Shall we thy guests   (2)
> Meet at those lyric feasts   (3)
> Made at the Sun,   (2)
> The Dog, the Triple Tun,   (3)
> Where we such clusters had   (3)
> As made us nobly wild, not mad;   (4)
> And yet each verse of thine   (3)
> Outdid the meat, outdid the frolic wine. (5)

The following examples illustrate respectively hexameter, heptameter, octameter, and nonameter.

Sweet is the treading of wine, and sweet the feet of the dove.
(Swinburne, *Hymn to Proserpine*) [1]

Inward and outward to northward and southward the beach-lines linger and curl.
(Lanier, *The Marshes of Glynn*) [2]

In the spring a livelier iris changes on the burnish'd dove.
(Tennyson, *Locksley Hall*)

Roman Virgil, thou that singest Ilion's lofty temples robed in fire.

(Tennyson, *To Virgil*)

In English verse the most common lines are trimeter, tetrameter, and pentameter. Monometer and dimeter, because of their brevity, tend to cramp the sense, particularly when rhyme is used. Lines longer than pentameter are unwieldy in English and, unless handled with great care, tend to break into two parts, each composed of

[1] By permission of Harper & Brothers.
[2] By permission of Charles Scribner's Sons.

fewer feet. Thus in metrical effect hexameter becomes the equivalent of two trimeters, heptameter the equivalent of a tetrameter and a trimeter, etc.

The foot, considered as a time interval, is normally composed of three elements: (1) an accented syllable which usually coincides with the metrical beat, (2) a varying number of unaccented syllables, and (3) the intervals of silence between sounds. It is a characteristic of speech that emphasis necessarily lengthens the time required for the pronunciation of a word or syllable. For example, observe the difference in time required for the pronunciation of the word "my" in the following two sentences: *"This* is my belief." "Although you hold otherwise, this is *my* belief." It therefore follows that the accented syllable of a foot actually consumes more time in pronunciation than the unaccented syllables.

The time value of unaccented syllables varies in proportion to the extent that they are slurred in common pronunciation, as well as in proportion to the difficulty or ease with which their combination of vowel and consonant sounds can be spoken. Similarly, both sound and sense combine to vary the length of pauses between spoken syllables. As a result, the character of a verse foot, thus composed of differing elements of sound and silence, admits of infinite variety.

The number of syllables normally appearing in a foot varies from one to four. Feet of but one syllable are comparatively rare. In such feet there is a lengthening of the spoken syllable as well as a pause to compensate for the missing unaccented syllables. The pause may be required by the sense or by the combination of consonant sounds, or by both, as in the following example. Observe that the first line is a trimeter.

> Break! break! break!
> On thy cold, grey stones, O sea.

Feet of four syllables (known as **quadruple meter**) are also rather rare. The reason is that such feet have a tendency to break in the middle into two feet, each containing two syllables. For the same reason even quadruple feet which do not break in half frequently have a *secondary accent* in addition to the normal primary accent. This may be illustrated by the following:

> When a felon's not engaged in his employment,
> Or maturing his felonious little plans,
> His capacity for innocent enjoyment
> Is just as great as any honest man's.
> (W. S. Gilbert, Song from *The Pirates of Penzance*) [3]

The most common verse feet contain either two or three syllables, one of which normally is accented and coincides with the metrical beat.

[The conventional symbol for an accented syllable is – ; that for an unaccented syllable is ⌣ . As a rough approximation, the time value of an unaccented syllable may be taken as about one-half that of an accented syllable.]

[3] From *The Savoy Operas*. By permission of The Macmillan Company.

Feet composed of two syllables (- ᵛ) constitute what is known as **duple meter.** The meter of the following lines from Browning's *Song* is duple:

> Nay, but you, who do not love her,
> Is she not pure gold, my mistress?

Feet composed of three syllables (- ᵛ ᵛ) constitute what is known as **triple meter,** as in these lines from Hood's *The Bridge of Sighs:*

> Take her up tenderly,
> Lift her with care;
> Fashioned so slenderly,
> Young, and so fair.

A third factor which enters into verse is known as **rhythmic movement.** If one considers unaccented syllables in relation to the accented syllables which they adjoin, it will be seen that they may structurally or logically either follow or precede the accented syllables. In the line, "Rarely, rarely comest thou," the unaccented syllables naturally belong with the preceding accented syllables, and produce what is known as a **falling rhythm.** On the other hand, in the line, "She danced along with vague, regardless eyes," it is obvious that the unaccented syllables belong with the following accented syllables. The rhythm thus mounts from the unaccented to the accented syllable and produces what is called **rising rhythm.**

To distinguish the different kinds of verse feet produced by the factors just discussed, the following conventional names are used: iambus, trochee, anapest, and dactyl. Two, it will be seen, apply to duple meter, and two to triple meter. Similarly, two apply to rising rhythm, and two to falling rhythm.

(1) The **iambus** (or **iamb**) is a foot of duple meter with a rising rhythm. (˘ -) The following illustrates iambic verse:

> A mind at peace with all below,
>   A heart whose love is innocent.
>   (Byron, *She Walks in*
>   *Beauty*)

(2) The **trochee** is a foot of duple meter with falling rhythm. (- ˘) The following illustrates trochaic verse:

> Souls of poets dead and gone,
> What Elysium have ye known,
> Happy field or mossy cavern,
> Choicer than the Mermaid Tavern?
>   (Keats, *Lines on the Mermaid*
>   *Tavern*)

(3) The **anapest** is a foot of triple meter with rising rhythm. (˘ ˘ -) The following line from Byron's *The Destruction of Sennacherib* is anapestic:

And the sheen of their spears was like stars on the sea.

(4) The **dactyl** is a foot of triple meter with falling rhythm. (- ˘ ˘) The following stanza, although not absolutely regular, illustrates the general character of dactyllic verse.

> Cannon to right of them,
> Cannon to left of them,

> Cannon in front of them
> Volley'd and thunder'd.
> (Tennyson, *The Charge of
> the Light Brigade*)

As has been said before, the distinguishing characteristic of verse is regular metrical pattern. Although certain variations may be introduced, general uniformity must be maintained or the pattern will be destroyed. Thus verse is described as iambic, trochaic, anapestic, or dactyllic with respect to *the predominant nature of the feet which compose the pattern.* The subtle rhythmic effects of poetry, however, are attained through variation within the pattern. That is, upon the regular metrical pattern is imposed a network of larger rhythms growing out of the sense and phraseology of the language used. These variations demand special consideration.

(1) *Variation in Number of Syllables*

One of the commonest variations is the substitution of a greater or less number of syllables for that normally expected of the foot. Apparently this amounts to a substitution of an anapest for an iambus, a dactyl for a trochee, or the reverse. Actually the important fact to observe is that the addition or suppression of an unaccented syllable does not lengthen or shorten the time value of the foot. The change lies in the use of syllables which by their very nature either accelerate or retard the pronunciation in such a manner that the time value of the foot may remain constant. This type of variation usually results in what has been called **duple-triple meter,** which may be illustrated by the following.

> Before the beginning of years
> > There came to the making of man
> Time, with a gift of tears;
> > Grief, with a glass that ran.
> > > (Swinburne, *Atalanta in Calydon*) [4]

Occasionally all unaccented syllables in a foot may be omitted. In such cases there is a compensating lengthening of the accented syllable plus a pause required either by sense or the peculiarities of adequate pronunciation. [See the example given above, p. 149.]

A special case of variation in the number of syllables occurs at the beginning and end of lines. Here occasionally may be added extra unaccented syllables not required by the meter. Such a practice is known as **anacrusis** when it occurs at the beginning, and **feminine ending** at the end of a line. The italicized syllables in the following, from Rossetti's *The Blessed Damozel*,[5] illustrate the practice:

> The blessed damozel leaned out
> > *From* the golden bar of Heav*en;*
> Her eyes were deeper than the depth
> > Of waters stilled at ev*en.*

Similarly certain initial or terminal syllables required by the meter may be omitted. This practice is known as **catalexis,** and a line so affected as catalectic. In the first

---

[4] By permission of Harper & Brothers.
[5] By permission of Little, Brown & Company.

of the following examples the third line is catalectic. In the second example the first two trochaic lines are cata-lectic, the last two regular, or a-catalectic.

> The year's at the spring,
> And day's at the morn;
> Morning's at seven;
> The hill-side's dew-pearled.
> > (Browning, *Pippa*
> > *Passes*)

> Music, when soft voices die,
> Vibrates in the memory—
> Odours, when sweet violets sicken,
> Live within the sense they quicken.
> > (Shelley, *To* ——)

(2) *Variation in Stress*

A more difficult, but most effective, variation often occurs in the number and distribution of accented syllables within the verse line. It has been mentioned that normally the metrical beat and the accented syllable coincide. It should be noted, however, that metrical beat and syllabic stress are two different things, which may or may not coincide. The metrical beat is constant and invariable. Syllabic accent normally does, but frequently may not, coincide with it. Thus there may be either more or fewer syllabic accents in a line than there are metrical beats. This variation may result from either of two situations.

Occasionally a metrical beat falls not upon a spoken sound but upon an interval of silence, just as in music the beat may fall upon a rest. Thus the number of accented syllables is diminished, *but the time value of the line has not been altered*. This situation occurs in the following iambic pentameter lines from *Macbeth:*

To-mórrow, (´) and to-mórrow, (´) and to-mórrow,
Créeps in this pétty páce from dáy to dáy,
To the lást sýllable (´) of recórded tíme.

Sometimes the time value of syllables within a foot is altered. For example, in the line, "O that this too too solid flesh would thaw," the foot "would thaw" is an iambus in which the syllable "thaw" has a time value approximately twice that of "would." This time relationship may be expressed numerically by the ratio 2 : 4. But it is obvious that the time value of such a foot may also be distributed so that the ratio becomes 3 : 3, and the value of both syllables becomes the same. In the line quoted above such a foot is provided by the syllables "too too." A foot of this character, in which both syllables have equal time value, is known as a **spondee.** But equal time distribution also tends to distribute the stress : that is, it both gives an accent to each syllable and lightens somewhat the stress upon each. Lines of verse which contain feet of this kind inevitably possess more accented syllables than metrical beats. A good example is provided by the following iambic pentameter lines from Milton's *Paradise Lost:*

. . . Through mány a dárk and dréary vále
They pássed, and mány a région doloróus,
O'er mány a frózen, mány a fiery Álp,
Ròcks, càves, làkes, fèns, bògs, dèns, and shádes of déath.

(3) *Variation in Phrase Rhythm*

This third variation is one, not of the verse foot, but of the rhythmic phrases which compose the line and the larger verse passage. Although metrical pattern is constructed with respect to the verse line, the phrase groups which make up the larger rhythms of verse are not. Accordingly, considerable rhythmic variety can be gained as phrasing diverges from normal line length. Phrasing is marked by the pauses in speech dictated by the sense, and is frequently indicated by punctuation.

When the sense of a phrase demands a pause at the end of a verse line, such a line is spoken of as an **end-stopped line.** When the sense of a phrase requires a continuous flow from one line to the next, such a line is called a **run-on line,** and the device is known as **enjambement.** Verse lines, moreover, may be broken internally by pauses demanded by the sense. Such a pause within the line is known as a **cæsura.**

By a skilful use of the cæsura, through shifting its position in the line, and by a judicious arrangement of run-on and end-stopped lines, most elaborate and pleasing rhythm effects can be superimposed upon what might otherwise be a metrical pattern so simple as to be monotonous. In the following selection from Wordsworth's *Tinturn Abbey,* note the variety of effects achieved by these means.

> For I have learned
> To look on nature, not as in the hour
> Of thoughtless youth; but hearing oftentimes
> The still, sad music of humanity,

Nor harsh nor grating, though of ample power
To chasten and subdue. And I have felt
A presence that disturbs me with the joy
Of elevated thoughts; a sense sublime
Of something far more deeply interfused,
Whose dwelling is the light of setting suns,
And the round ocean and the living air,
And the blue sky, and in the mind of man:
A motion and a spirit, that impels
All thinking things, all objects of all thought,
And rolls through all things.

II. TONE COLOR

The second contribution which sound makes to the quality of poetry is known as tone color. **Tone color** is the pattern of related sound values woven by language artistically arranged. As rhythm refers to the sense of movement in language, so tone color refers to the tonal qualities inherent in vowel and consonant combinations.

Tone color depends for its effect upon two important properties of sound as found in speech. The first is the natural pitch of vowel sounds. [Observe the difference in pitch between the vowel sounds in the following pairs of words: *brood, thud; bleed, blood; wring, wrong.*] The second is the emotional response either consciously or unconsciously associated with different sounds. Thus the consonants *l, m,* and *r,* for instance, produce a sense of ease, smoothness and pleasure, whereas the consonants *b, k,* and *t* create a sense of harshness, abruptness, and difficulty. Further observe the difference in emotional reaction to the ejaculatory sounds "oh!" and "ha!" In different combinations, a wide variety of emotional responses can be suggested by mere sounds alone entirely divorced from sense. A world of doleful implication is contained in the mere sound of the word "moan," while the word "squeak" by its very sound conveys the shrill, sharp, high-pitched brittleness of the word's meaning.

Tone color imparts to language the texture of tonal quality. It is to speech what the blend of color is to painting or the timbre of various instruments is to an orchestra. In general it may be used as an incidental embellishment or to reënforce sense with sound.

In the first case, the skilful modulations of sound may be used to play a verbal melody for the ear. Thus may be created a verse music pleasurable in itself, irrespective of meaning. It is thus analogous to an appropriate musical setting for the poem. Consider the pure musical value of the following excerpt from Swinburne's *Atalanta in Calydon:* [6]

> For winter's rains and ruins are over,
>   And all the season of snows and sins;
> The days dividing lover and lover,
>   The light that loses, the night that wins;
> And time remembered is grief forgotten,
> And frosts are slain and flowers begotten,
> And in green underwood and cover
>   Blossom by blossom the spring begins.

A second effective use of tone color is to reënforce the sense of a passage. That is, the resources of sound are utilized either to give an echo of the meaning of words,

[6] By permission of Harper & Brothers.

or to induce sensuously a mood appropriate to the subject under consideration. Observe how the sense of the following passage from Tennyson's *Song of the Lotos-Eaters* is enriched by the tonal accompaniment.

> How sweet it were, hearing the downward stream,
> With half-shut eyes ever to seem
> Falling asleep in a half-dream!
> To dream and dream, like yonder amber light,
> Which will not leave the myrrh-bush on the height;
> To hear each other's whisper'd speech;
> Eating the Lotos day by day,
> To watch the crisping ripples on the beach,
> And tender curving lines of creamy spray;
> To lend our hearts and spirits wholly
> To the influence of mild-minded melancholy;
> To muse and brood and live again in memory,
> With those old faces of our infancy
> Heap'd over with a mound of grass,
> Two handfuls of white dust, shut in an urn of brass!

A specialized variety of such tone color is known as onomatopœia. **Onomatopœia** (a Greek word which means "name-making") in its narrowest sense means the use of a word the sound of which reproduces its meaning. [Such words as *buzz, twitter, hum* are onomatopoetic.] In a larger sense, onomatopœia is the use of language in such a manner as to illustrate meaning with sound. An excellent example is provided by the following lines from Tennyson's *Morte d'Arthur*.

> Dry clash'd his harness in the icy caves
> And barren chasms, and all to left and right
> The bare black cliff clang'd round him, as he based

> His feet on juts of slippery crag that rang
> Sharp-smitten with the dint of armed heels—
> And on a sudden, lo! the level lake,
> And the long glories of the winter moon.

Although verbal music in general depends primarily upon the sequence of vowel and consonant sounds, certain of the specialized devices of tone color have a structural value in addition to pure sound. Such devices, besides contributing to the tonal harmony, help to unite organically the various elements of the poem. The most important of these specialized devices are repetition, rhyme, alliteration, and assonance.

The **repetition** of a word or group of words not only gives emphasis, but frequently produces unusual sound effects and shifting patterns of meaning. A rather obvious example may be drawn from Poe's *Ulalume*.

> The skies they were ashen and sober;
>　The leaves they were crispèd and sere,
>　The leaves they were withering and sere;
> It was night in the lonesome October
>　Of my most immemorial year;
> It was hard by the dim lake of Auber,
>　In the misty mid region of Weir:
> It was down by the dank tarn of Auber,
>　In the ghoul-haunted woodland of Weir.

A common type of repetition is the refrain. A **refrain** is a word, phrase, line, or stanza repeated throughout a poem either intact or with slight modification. The refrain may be either an integral part of the poem or merely related to it in spirit or mood. Its effect is to give emphasis, a pleasing sense of musical "return," or an impression of the organic unity of the central theme. Two stanzas of the old ballad *Lord Randal* illustrate one use of the refrain.

"O where hae ye been, Lord Randal, my son?
 O where hae ye been, my handsome young man?"
"I hae been to the wild wood; mother, make my bed soon,
 For I'm weary wi hunting, and fain wald lie down."

"Where gat ye your dinner, Lord Randal, my son?
 Where gat ye your dinner, my handsome young man?"
"I din'd wi my true love; mother, make my bed soon,
 For I'm weary wi hunting, and fain wald lie down."

Rhyme (also spelled *rime*) is the matching of syllables the sounds of which, except for initial modification, are identical. It is one of the most characteristic devices of modern English verse. Not only does rhyme please the ear with a novel effect of similarity in dissimilarity, but structurally it links the various parts of the poem and marks off the units of which it is composed. Of rhyme there are several important kinds.

(1) *Perfect Rhyme*

Perfect rhyme is rhyme in which the vowel sound of the accented syllable and all sounds of any subsequent syllables of two or more rhymed words correspond exactly, but in which the sounds preceding the accented vowel differ.

> Sweet day, so cool, so calm, so *bright,*
>   The bridal of the earth and *sky,*

> The dew shall weep thy fall to-*night*,
> For thou must *die*.
>   (Herbert, *Virtue*)

[Rhyme, it should be noted, depends upon sound, not spelling. Thus the following are perfect rhymes: *great, eight; go, slow.* On the other hand, the following are not perfect rhymes: *great, heat; eight, height; go, to; slow, plow.*]

(2) *Imperfect Rhyme*

Imperfect rhyme is rhyme in which the correspondence described above is not exact but approximate. Its use is accepted with certain words which are poor in exact rhymes, and occasionally with others for the purpose of achieving subtle sound effects.

> Only reapers, reaping *early*
> In among the bearded *barley,*
> Hear a song that echoes *cheerly*
> From the river winding *clearly,*
>   Down to tower'd Camelot.
>   (Tennyson, *The Lady of*
>   *Shalott*)

[In reading poets of the past, one must take care not to interpret as imperfect rhyme the matching of words which once constituted a perfect rhyme but since have altered their pronunciation. Pope's rhyming of *join* with *line* and *tea* with *obey* are examples. The same caution applies to words which have a different pronunciation in England and America.]

(3) *Identical Rhyme*

Identical rhyme is rhyme in which the paired syllables are identical in sound but different in meaning. Although

admitted in older poetry, modern English verse avoids
identical rhyme as a blemish.

> Soft and strong and loud and *light,*
> Very sound of very *light*
> Heard from morning's rosiest height,
> When the soul of all de*light*
> Fills a child's clear laughter.
> (Swinburne, *A Child's
> Laughter*) [7]

(4) *Apparent Rhyme*

Apparent rhyme, or, as it is sometimes called, *eye-rhyme,* is rhyme which depends not upon correspondence of sound but of spelling. In many cases it represents conscious perpetuation of a rhyme once perfect but now false because of change in pronunciation. Its principal use is in connection with words poor in rhyme equivalents.

> The kettle-drum, and far-heard clarinet,
> Affray his ears, though but in dying *tone:*—
> The hall door shuts again, and all the noise is *gone.*
> (Keats, *The Eve of St. Agnes*)

Rhyme most frequently occurs at the end of a line of
verse. In such a position it is known as **tail rhyme.** It
may, however, occur within the line and thus tend to
break the line into smaller units. Such rhyme is known
as **internal rhyme.**

Ah, distinctly I *remember* it was in the bleak *December,*
And each separate dying *ember* wrought its ghost upon the
floor.

> (Poe, *The Raven*)

[7] By permission of Harper & Brothers.

Since rhyme involves the correspondence of both accented syllables and subsequent syllables, rhyme therefore may include one or more syllables of a word. When the rhyme consists of only the accented final syllable of a word, such rhyme is called **masculine rhyme.** Rhyme which includes an accented syllable followed by a single unaccented syllable is called **feminine** or **double rhyme.** When two unaccented syllables follow the accented syllable, the rhyme is known as **triple rhyme.** Because of the difficulty in finding perfect triple rhymes without resorting to grotesque ingenuity, such rhymes usually tend to lighten the tone of verse and are rarely used except for deliberate comic or grotesque effect. Examples of the three kinds of rhyme follow.

> At last he rose, and twitched his mantle blue:
> To-morrow to fresh woods and pastures new.
> (Milton, *Lycidas*)

> This is a spray the bird clung to,
>   Making it blossom with pleasure,
> Ere the high tree-top she sprung to,
>   Fit for her nest and her treasure.
> (Browning, *Misconceptions*)

> When all night long a chap remains
>   On sentry-go, to chase monotony
> He exercises of his brains—
>   That is, assuming that he's got any.
> (W. S. Gilbert, Song from
>   *Iolanthe*) [8]

[8] From *The Savoy Operas.* By permission of The Macmillan Company.

Alliteration is really a variety of rhyme. It is to the beginning of words what tail rhyme is to the end, and thus is sometimes called *beginning rhyme*. Alliteration is exact correspondence in the initial sounds of accented syllables. Observe that alliteration, like rhyme, applies to *sound,* not spelling, and further that it applies only to *accented syllables.* Thus the following words alliterate perfectly: *sure, sharp, chaise; chorus, king, call, quell,* and *acquaint.* Words like *unknown* and *uncouth, indifferent* and *invincible* do not alliterate. The following line illustrates a simple alliterative pattern.

*M*aiden most *b*eautiful, *m*other most *b*ountiful, *l*ady of *l*ands.
(Swinburne, *The Song of the Standard*)

Assonance, strictly speaking, is identity of vowel sounds and dissimilarity of consonant sounds. Thus the words *right, clime; shame, chain,* are examples of assonance. In a broader sense, assonance is any relationship of sounds not close enough to be rhyme, and yet sufficiently close to suggest immediate similarity. Sometimes there is merely a variation of vowel sounds in syllables otherwise substantially the same. For example: *stun, stone; gone, alone.* This broader usage is sometimes known as **consonance.** Occasionally assonance is substituted for rhyme; more commonly it is used as an incidental embellishment. As such, it is one of the most valuable components of tone color. Consider its effect in the following examples.

When I have *fears* that I may *cease* to *be*
Before my pen has *glean'd* my *teeming* brain . . .
(Keats, *When I Have Fears*)

> I've known her from an ample *nation*
>   Choose *one;*
> Then close the valves of her *attention*
>   Like *stone*.
>
> (E. Dickinson, The Soul
Selects) [9]

III. Structural Patterns of Verse

The final distinguishing forms which different kinds of poetry assume depend upon two factors. The first of these is the structural pattern of verse selected by the poet as his vehicle of expression. The second is the purpose of the poem. Theoretically the two are intimately related, and traditional practice has frequently established certain verse patterns as most appropriate to certain purposes. Such is the case in the use of blank verse for poetic drama or long narrative. Nevertheless, for the sake of clarity and simplicity, it is best to consider the two factors separately.

In our discussion of meter we considered verse with respect only to the single line. We now deal with the larger problem of the arrangement of lines with respect to the entire poem. In such an arrangement two sharply defined conceptions of versification are to be noted: regular versification and irregular or free versification. Since the former is traditionally characteristic of most English verse and alone possesses a formal technique, it will be discussed in detail. The latter, since by its very nature

[9] From "The Poems of Emily Dickinson," centenary edition, edited by Martha Dickinson Bianchi and Alfred Leete Hampson. Reprinted by permission of Little, Brown & Company.

it is a revolt against formal technique and is therefore highly individualistic in method, will be discussed more briefly.

The structure of regular verse is of two distinct orders. In one, the arrangement of lines is such that the verse flows continuously from the beginning of the poem to the end with only such breaks as are dictated by the sense. Such verse may be called **continuous** or **non-stanzaic verse.** In the other, the verse progresses through a series of uniform groups of lines, each complete in itself and distinct from the others. Such verse is called **stanzaic verse.**

NON-STANZAIC VERSE

Non-stanzaic verse may be found in either short or long poems. In long poems it is frequently divided, by the indentation of lines, into sections which are known as **verse paragraphs.** Such divisions are similar to the paragraphs of prose. Very long poems are often further divided into **books** or **cantos,** which correspond to the chapters of a volume of prose. The principal kinds of non-stanzaic verse are discussed below.

Blank verse is unrhymed iambic pentameter verse. It is by far the favorite English verse form for sustained poetic composition. It is the standard expression for poetic drama and for lengthy narrative and reflective poetry. It is the verse of Shakespeare's plays, Milton's *Paradise Lost,* Wordsworth's *Prelude,* Tennyson's *Idylls of the King,* and many of Browning's monologues. Its virtue is its flexibility, which permits the widest variety of verse effects. It may be illustrated by the following lines from Bryant's *Thanatopsis*: [10]

> So live, that when thy summons comes to join
> The innumerable caravan, which moves
> To that mysterious realm, where each shall take
> His chamber in the silent halls of death,
> Thou go not, like the quarry-slave at night,
> Scourged to his dungeon, but, sustained and soothed
> By an unfaltering trust, approach thy grave,
> Like one who wraps the drapery of his couch
> About him, and lies down to pleasant dreams.

Rhymed couplets are contiguous pairs of lines which rhyme. For sustained poetry they provide something of the free sweep of blank verse with the additional embellishment, and check, of rhyme. The two favorite couplets of English verse are the tetrameter and pentameter couplets. These, since they are usually found in either iambic or trochaic meter, are usually referred to by names which indicate the number of syllables to the line.

The **octosyllabic couplet** (either iambic or trochaic tetrameter) is a favorite for narrative and descriptive verse. Its movement is fluent, light, graceful, and often rapid. It has been found most useful for humorous and burlesque effects, as in Butler's *Hudibras* and Burns's *Tam o' Shanter*. It is the meter of Milton's *L'Allegro* and *Il Penseroso*, Marvell's *To His Coy Mistress*, Morris's *The Haystack in the Floods*, Whittier's *Snow-Bound*, and

[10] By permission of D. Appleton-Century Company.

several of the verse tales of Scott and Byron. The following example is from Scott's *The Lady of the Lake*.

> The stag at eve had drunk his fill,
> Where danced the moon on Monan's rill,
> And deep his midnight lair had made
> In lone Glenartney's hazel shade.

The **decasyllabic couplet** (iambic pentameter) next to blank verse is the most popular non-stanzaic form of verse, particularly for descriptive and didactic poetry. It occurs in two forms known respectively as open and closed couplets. **Open couplets** are those in which the sense and rhythm flow without interruption from couplet to couplet. **Closed couplets** are those in which both sense and rhythm are restricted to complete expression within the couplet. The following are open couplets:

> Stop and consider! life is but a day;
> A fragile dew-drop on its perilous way
> From a tree's summit; a poor Indian's sleep
> While his boat hastens to the monstrous steep
> Of Montmorenci. . . .
>
> (Keats, *Sleep and Poetry*)

The following are closed couplets:

> Soft is the strain when Zephyr gently blows,
> And the smooth stream in smoother numbers flows;
> But when loud surges lash the sounding shore,
> The hoarse, rough verse should like the torrent roar:
> When Ajax strives some rock's vast weight to throw,
> The line too labours, and the words move slow:
> Not so, when swift Camilla scours the plain,
> Flies o'er the unbending corn, and skims along the main.
>
> (Pope, *Essay on Criticism*)

The closed decasyllabic couplet is often called the **heroic couplet.** In this form, during the later seventeenth and the eighteenth centuries, the couplet became the standard of most poetic expression. It is particularly adapted to pointed, witty, elegant and epigrammatic effects; and perhaps reached its perfection in the work of Alexander Pope. In verse composed of heroic couplets two variations commonly appear. The first is the substitution of a triplet for a couplet. A **triplet** is a group of three lines with the same rhyme. The second variation is the substitution of an Alexandrine for one of the regular pentameter lines of the couplet. An **Alexandrine** is a line of iambic hexameter verse. Although uncommon in English verse, the Alexandrine is the standard line of French verse, and derives its name from its use in French mediæval romances dealing with Alexander the Great. An example of its use in connection with heroic couplets occurs in the last line of the selection from Pope immediately above.

The foregoing are the most important non-stanzaic forms. In addition, two less important forms occasionally are found in English verse. These are known as terza rima and dactyllic hexameters.

Terza rima is continuous iambic pentameter verse arranged in **tercets** (groups of three lines) in such a manner that in each tercet the first and third lines rhyme, while the intervening line rhymes with the first and third lines of the following tercet. The conclusion of each section of a poem in terza rima is a group of four lines rhymed alternately. Terza rima is the verse form of

Dante's *Divine Comedy*. Although it appears rarely in
English poetry, it may be found in *The Defence of
Guenevere* by William Morris, and in modified form in
Shelley's *Ode to the West Wind* and Browning's *The
Statue and the Bust*.

> "All I have said is truth, by Christ's dear tears."
> She would not speak another word, but stood
> Turned sideways, listening, like a man who hears
>
> His brother's trumpet sounding through the wood
> Of his foes' lances. She leaned eagerly,
> And gave a slight spring sometimes, as she could
>
> At last hear something really; joyfully
> Her cheek grew crimson, as the headlong speed
> Of the roan charger drew all men to see,
> The knight who came was Launcelot at good need.
>   (Morris, *The Defence of Guenevere*) [11]

Dactyllic hexameter verse is the great classic verse
of Homer's *Iliad* and *Odyssey* and of Virgil's *Æneid*.
Since it is a form not easily adaptable to English verse,
its appearance in English poetry is usually something of
a tour de force in imitation of the ancient form. Perhaps
the best known example of the form in English is Longfellow's *Evangeline*. The following example is from the
same poet's *The Courtship of Miles Standish*.[12]

But as he warmed and glowed, in his simple and eloquent
    language,
Quite forgetful of self, and full of the praise of his rival,

[11] By permission of Longmans, Green & Co.
[12] By permission of Houghton Mifflin Company.

Archly the maiden smiled, and, with eyes overrunning with
    laughter,
Said, in a tremulous voice, "Why don't you speak for your-
    self, John?"

STANZAIC VERSE

The second important regular verse structure is that of
stanzaic or strophic verse. A **stanza** is a group of lines,
so arranged as to form an invariable pattern, which constitutes a complete unit in the development of a poem.
Although rhyme is not essential, in English verse rhyme
is customarily used to reënforce the pattern.

Strictly speaking, a **strophe** is one of the divisions of
an ode (see p. 195). In its more extended use in English
verse, a strophe is a group of lines constituting a unit in
the development of a poem, but not arranged in an invariable pattern.

Although stanzas may be constructed in many ways,
the great majority are combinations of three common
elements: the single line, the couplet, and the quatrain
(or group of four lines). In structural combinations of
these elements English verse is exceedingly versatile.
English poets have constantly experimented with new and
ingenious stanza forms. Indeed, it may be said to be characteristic of English poetry that it prefers individual experimentation to the acceptance of standardized forms. As
a result, many of the conventional stanzas of English
verse represent imitations or adaptations of foreign
forms. But, in addition, the appropriateness of certain
native stanza forms to particular purposes has established
them as familiar and important English stanzas. In the

following discussion no attempt is made to indicate the almost limitless stanza forms which experiment has devised; the stanzas described are only those which have been used by a number of poets and have established themselves as familiar units of expression.

[For convenience in describing stanza forms it has become conventional to use certain symbols. The lines of a stanza are represented by the letters of the alphabet, the initial letters indicating rhymed lines and the terminal letters unrhymed lines. The number of feet in the line is indicated by a superior number to the right of the letter. Thus a pentameter quatrain rhymed alternately is represented thus: $a^5 b^5 a^5 b^5$. A quatrain of alternate tetrameter and trimeter, with rhyme in the second and fourth lines but no rhyme in the first and third, is indicated thus: $x^4 a^3 y^4 a^3$.]

Although couplets and triplets are occasionally used as separate stanzas, such use is rare. By far the simplest and most popular stanza is the four-line stanza, or **quatrain**. Among a number of forms which the quatrain may take, several may be distinguished.

(1) The **common meter quatrain,** or, as it is frequently named, the *ballad stanza,* consists of four lines of alternate tetrameter and trimeter, with rhyme in the second and fourth lines, and rhyme optional in the others. (It may be symbolized: $a^4 b^3 a^4 b^3$, or $x^4 a^3 y^4 a^3$.) It is the easiest and simplest of all stanzas, and is the common stanza of many ballads and most doggerel.

> About, about, in reel and rout
> The death-fires danced at night;
> The water, like a witch's oils,

> Burnt green, and blue, and white.
>   (Coleridge, *The Rime of the*
>   *Ancient Mariner*)

(2) The **short meter quatrain** is similar to the stanza just described except that all lines are trimeter. ($a^3 b^3 a^3 b^3$, or $x^3 a^3 y^3 a^3$.)

> Strew on her roses, roses,
>   And never a spray of yew.
> In quiet she reposes:
>   Ah! would that I did too.
>   (Arnold, *Requiescat*)

(3) The **long meter quatrain** is similar to the two stanzas described above except that all lines are tetrameter. ($a^4 b^4 a^4 b^4$, or $x^4 a^4 y^4 a^4$.)

> My love is of a birth as rare
>   As 'tis for object strange and high:
> It was begotten by Despair
> Upon Impossibility.
>   (Marvell, *The Definition of*
>   *Love*)

(4) The **heroic** or **elegiac stanza** is four lines of alternately rhymed iambic pentameter ($a^5 b^5 a^5 b^5$). Its two names are derived from the fact that in the late seventeenth century it was used in narrative and descriptive poems of a lofty, heroic nature, and later was used to approximate in English the Latin elegiac verse of Tibullus.

> The boast of heraldry, the pomp of power,
> And all that beauty, all that wealth e'er gave

Await alike th' inevitable hour :—
The paths of glory lead but to the grave.
(Gray, *Elegy Written in a Country
Churchyard*)

(5) The **In Memoriam stanza** is an iambic tetrameter quatrain rhymed *a b b a*. It derives its name from its use in Tennyson's great elegy, *In Memoriam,* from which the following lines are taken.

> Again at Christmas did we weave
> The holly round the Christmas hearth;
> The silent snow possessed the earth;
> And calmly fell our Christmas eve.

(6) The **Rubáiyát stanza** is an iambic pentameter quatrain rhymed *a a x a*. It derives its name from its use in Edward Fitzgerald's translation of the *Rubáiyát* of Omar Khayyám, from which the following example is taken.

> The Moving Finger writes; and, having writ,
> Moves on: nor all your Piety nor Wit
> Shall lure it back to cancel half a Line,
> Nor all your Tears wash out a Word of it.

Although many five-line stanzas, or **quintains,** occur, none is sufficiently standardized to require special attention. Among **sexains,** or six-line stanzas, two without name may be distinguished by their rhyme scheme. These common stanzas are found, in various meters, rhymed as follows:

(1) *a b a b c c* (a quatrain completed by a couplet)

> I wandered lonely as a cloud
> That floats on high o'er vales and hills,

> When all at once I saw a crowd,
> A host of golden daffodils;
> Beside the lake, beneath the trees,
> Fluttering and dancing in the breeze.
>> (Wordsworth, *I Wandered Lonely
>> as a Cloud*)

(2) *a b a b a b* (or *x a y a z a*)

> The sun was gone now; the curled moon
>> Was like a little feather
> Fluttering far down the gulf; and now
>> She spoke through the still weather.
> Her voice was like the voice the stars
>> Had when they sang together.
>> (Rosetti, *The Blessed Damozel*) [13]

The only important seven-line stanza is the rime royal, introduced into English poetry in the fourteenth century by Geoffrey Chaucer. **Rime royal** ("a royall kinde of verse," as the poet Gascoigne calls it) is an iambic pentameter stanza rhymed *a b a b b c c.*

> Then in the sunset's flush they went aloft,
> And unbent sails in that most lovely hour,
> When the light gentles and the wind is soft,
> And beauty in the heart breaks like a flower.
> Working aloft they saw the mountain tower,
> Snow to the peak; they heard the launch-men shout;
> And bright along the bay the lights came out.
>> (Masefield, *Dauber*) [14]

The principal **octaves,** or eight-line stanzas, are two in number, known as double quatrains and ottava rima.

[13] By permission of Little, Brown & Company.
[14] By permission of The Macmillan Company.

Double quatrains, as the name implies, constitute a stanza formed of two quatrains, usually with alternate rhymes (*a b a b c d c d*).

> When the lamp is shattered,
> The light in the dust lies dead;
> When the cloud is scattered,
> The rainbow's glory is shed;
> When the lute is broken,
> Sweet tones are remembered not;
> When the lips have spoken,
> Loved accents are soon forgot.
>   (Shelley, *Lines*)

Ottava rima is an iambic pentameter stanza borrowed from the Italian and rhymed *a b a b a b c c*. The stanza is admirable for sustained narrative or description, and has been used for satire by Byron in *Don Juan*. From that poem is taken the following example.

> Ave Maria! blessed be the hour!
> The time, the clime, the spot, where I so oft
> Have felt the moment in its fullest power
> Sink o'er the earth so beautiful and soft,
> While swung the deep bell in the distant tower,
> Or the faint dying day-hymn stole aloft,
> And not a breath crept through the rosy air,
> And yet the forest leaves seem'd stirr'd with prayer.

Of longer stanza forms only two need special mention: the Spenserian stanza and the sonnet. The **Spenserian stanza** is a nine-line stanza rhymed *a b a b b c b c c.* The first eight lines are iambic pentameter; the last line is an iambic hexameter, or Alexandrine. The stanza was invented by the poet Edmund Spenser for use in *The Faerie Queene,* and since has been popular with a number of poets. Its flexibility and its resources for rich description and verbal harmony have made it excellent for sustained poetry. As a result, it ranks next to blank verse and rhymed couplets as a medium for long poems.

> The One remains, the many change and pass;
> Heaven's light forever shines, Earth's shadows fly;
> Life, like a dome of many-coloured glass,
> Stains the white radiance of Eternity,
> Until Death tramples it to fragments.—Die,
> If thou wouldst be with that which thou dost seek!
> Follow where all is fled!—Rome's azure sky,
> Flowers, ruins, statues, music, words are weak
> The glory they transfuse with fitting truth to speak.
> (Shelley, *Adonais*)

The **sonnet** is both a stanza and an independent form of poetry. Because of this fact, detailed discussion of the sonnet is postponed until its proper place among the forms of verse. (See p. 196.) As for the mere external form, the sonnet is a stanza of fourteen iambic pentameter lines rhymed usually in accordance with one of the two following schemes: *a b b a a b b a c d e c d e* (considerable freedom is allowed in the arrangement of the rhymes of the last six lines), or *a b a b c d c d e f e f g g.* For examples see the later discussion, pp. 197 and 198.

FREE VERSE

Free verse (or, as it is frequently called, *vers libre*) is a form which endeavors to achieve the characteristic

effects of poetry without adherence to the conventional
restrictions of regular verse. In general, it represents an
effort to explore the rather indeterminate zone which
separates prose from verse. Frequently it results from
an imitation of alien verse forms which are based upon
metrical principles different from those of regular English
verse.

Free verse by its very nature is unconventional and
individualistic. Fundamentally the taste and intention of
the individual poet are the sole standards of technique.
At times the result is genuine poetry of a unique and
almost indefinable quality; at others, the result is merely
bad prose. Whatever the result, however, it is obvious
that the very nature of free verse precludes any definite
codification of its technique.

Certain very general principles, nevertheless, may be
distinguished, which produce recognizable varieties of
free verse. The most important of these are:

(1) *Verse of Irregular Line Pattern*

Vers libre, as a French experimental form, originally
meant, as its name indicates, merely freedom in varying
the length of verse lines. Otherwise it remains metrically
regular. As such, it is the oldest English form of free
verse. Its characteristic features are regularity of meter,
irregularity of line length, strophic rather than stanzaic
structure, and usually absence of rhyme. It is illustrated
in such poems as Arnold's *Philomela,* Christina Rossetti's
Goblin Market, Henley's *London Voluntaries,* and the
choruses from Milton's *Samson Agonistes.* The following

lines from W. E. Henley's *Margaritæ Sorori*[15] illustrate
the form.

> The smoke ascends
> In a rosy-and-golden haze. The spires
> Shine, and are changed. In the valley
> Shadows rise. The lark sings on. The sun,
> Closing his benediction,
> Sinks, and the darkening air
> Thrills with a sense of the triumphing night—
> Night with her train of stars
> And her great gift of sleep.

(2) *Verse of Irregular Rhythm*

The most common kind of modern free verse is that
which strives for subtle rhythmic effects through avoidance of the conventional regularity of meter. Such verse
derives from a theory, first, that conventional meter is
arbitrary and associated with traditional poetic subjects,
whereas new subjects demand fresh rhythms; and, second,
that each poetic subject holds within itself, and implies
inevitably, its own distinctive rhythmic expression. The
characteristic features of this form are irregularity of
line length, absence of rhyme, either continuous or
strophic structure, and substitution of cadence, or rhythmic modulation, for regular meter. In English verse its
first important exponent was the American, Walt Whitman. During the twentieth century it has been widely
cultivated by a variety of poets, and may be found illustrated in many of the poems of Stephen Crane, Amy
Lowell, Carl Sandburg, John Gould Fletcher, Robinson

[15] By permission of Charles Scribner's Sons.

Jeffers, and T. S. Eliot. From Whitman's *When Lilacs Last in the Dooryard Bloom'd* may be chosen an example.

> Come, lovely and soothing Death,
> Undulate round the world, serenely arriving, arriving,
> In the day, in the night, to all, to each,
> Sooner or later, delicate Death.
>
> Prais'd be the fathomless universe,
> For life and joy, and for objects and knowledge curious;
> And for love, sweet love— But praise! praise! praise!
> For the sure-enwinding arms of cool-enfolding Death.[16]

(3) *Verse of Graphic Emphasis*

A third variety of free verse is concerned not so much with the aural appeal of its rhythm as with the visual appeal of its arrangement in print. That is, pure sound effects are subordinated to logical relationships and meaning, and the printed version of the poem represents a diagram intended to suggest the relation of the various ideas and expressions of the poem to each other, as well as the relative distribution of emphasis. Outwardly such verse has the familiar absence of rhyme, freedom of line arrangement, and irregularity of rhythm; but in addition it practices an eccentricity of arrangement designed to throw into relief certain elements of the poem, sharply emphasize others, and in general indicate the various time and space relationships between the individual parts of the poem. The method is frankly an experimental one, and

[16] From "When Lilacs Last in the Dooryard Bloom'd," from *Leaves of Grass* by Walt Whitman, reprinted with permission from the publishers, Doubleday, Doran and Company, Inc.

frequently the result remains more of an ingenious experiment than a work of art. Varied examples of the method may be found especially in the poems of E. E. Cummings, Alfred Kreymborg, Ezra Pound, and William Carlos Williams, and to a less exaggerated degree among the poems of Amy Lowell, Carl Sandburg, H. D. (Hilda Doolittle), Hart Crane, Archibald MacLeish, and many other modern poets. The following rather extreme example is given because it throws into relief the characteristics of the method:

in Just-
spring   when the world is mud-
luscious the little
lame baloonman

whistles   far   and wee

and eddieandbill come
running from marbles and
piracies and it's
spring

when the world is puddle-wonderful

the queer
old baloonman whistles
far   and   wee
and bettyandisbel come dancing
from hop-scotch and jump-rope and

it's
spring
and
      the

            goat-footed

baloonman   whistles
far
and
wee
(E. E. Cummings, Chanson Innocent) [17]

Somewhat analogous to this form of free verse, but more chastened in its method, is the technique usually employed in **imagist verse.** Briefly, the ideal of imagism is to present through the medium of verse, with absolute accuracy of detail and coloring and sculptural precision of outline, a picture or image. In its verse technique sound values are practically eliminated. Its technique is adapted to give emphasis to visual pattern and design, to suggest spatial relationships, and to indicate the harmonies of mass, outline and color. A few lines from *Oread* by H. D. (Hilda Doolittle) will illustrate the method.

Whirl up, sea—
Whirl your pointed pines.
Splash your great pines
On our rocks.
Hurl your green over us—
Cover us with your pools of fir.[18]

IV. Types and Forms of Verse

The ultimate forms of English verse are seldom arbitrary or conventional. As has been stated before, the English poet usually creates or adapts his form to fit

[17] Reprinted from E. E. Cummings, *Tulips and Chimneys,* through the courtesy of Albert & Charles Boni, Inc.
[18] By permission of Liveright Publishing Corporation.

his subject so that the final blending of the two may appear unique. In other words, instead of thrusting his Muse into ready-made garments, he prefers to tailor her raiment to fit her individual figure. The obvious result is that an endeavor to describe with any completeness the multitude of English verse forms becomes so diffuse as to be fruitless. On the other hand, a limited number of forms have become sufficiently crystallized and popular to warrant description. It is a further verification of the native English practice in poetry that nearly all of these special forms are of foreign origin and have been imported for English imitation and adaptation. These will be discussed in their proper place below.

The true determining factors in English verse form are structural pattern and the purpose toward which the poem is directed. Structural pattern has been discussed above. But the repeated use of specific verse patterns for specific purposes has given rise to certain varieties of verse which can be recognized, which have received names, and which do possess, after a fashion, a sort of loose form.

With respect to purpose and use, poetry may be, and actually has been, well-nigh universal in scope. The difference between prose and poetry is to be found in the specialized effects which each strives for, and in the technical means used to achieve those effects, rather than in the general uses to which each is put.

Specifically, poetry may be used to describe a scene, to tell a story, to present a dramatic incident, to set forth an emotion or attitude in terms of song, or to expound an idea. With these uses are associated certain types of poetry known respectively as descriptive, narrative, dramatic, lyric, and didactic poetry. But these types, it must be understood, are not mutually exclusive. As a matter of fact, the terms are more useful for convenience in classification than for purposes of practical description. For a poem rarely is representative of one type alone; usually it combines the methods and features of several. For convenience it is classified according to the type which is predominant.

DESCRIPTIVE VERSE

Descriptive verse, although common enough, rarely exists as a type sufficient unto itself. Usually its use is subservient to some larger purpose. Nevertheless pure decription plays a major part in such poems as Coleridge's *Kubla Khan,* Keats's *Ode on a Grecian Urn,* Lanier's *The Marshes of Glynn,* Wordsworth's *The Solitary Reaper,* Swinburne's *A Forsaken Garden,* as well as in many of Rossetti's sonnets and in large sections of Byron's *Childe Harold.* The only important specialized form of descriptive verse is the idyl.

An **idyl** is a descriptive poem designed to present an idealized picture of rural life. As the definition indicates, the idyl is not, strictly speaking, a poetic form at all. It is, rather, a kind of poetry determined by content and general atmosphere. Often it is combined with the pastoral mode. The English idyl is a more or less remote echo of the idyls of Theocritus and Virgil. Modern idyls are Tennyson's *The Brook* and Whittier's *Snow-Bound.*

Tennyson's *Idylls of the King,* while retaining the idealization and elaborate description, abandon the characteristic rustic note.

Narrative verse, on the other hand, is one of the most popular poetic types. But as the forms of prose fiction are plastic and not very definite, so the forms of narrative verse are exceedingly variable. Apart from the differences in medium and artistic intention, prose narrative and verse narrative are quite similar. Indeed, what has been said of the technique and forms of the one is generally true of the other. Thus there is the **metrical romance,** differing from the prose romance chiefly in that the one is poetry and the other prose. Such are Spenser's *The Faerie Queene,* Tennyson's *Idylls of the King,* Scott's *The Lady of the Lake,* and Keats's *The Eve of St. Agnes.* There are **verse tales** such as Longfellow's *Tales of a Wayside Inn,* Noyes's *Tales of the Mermaid Tavern,* Wordsworth's *Michael,* Burns's *Tam o' Shanter,* and Byron's *Mazeppa* and *The Bride of Abydos.* There are even occasional **verse novels** such as Browning's *The Ring and the Book* or Stephen Vincent Benét's *John Brown's Body.*

Although the general forms of narrative verse are somewhat indefinite, certain structural patterns of verse have become popularly associated with the type. For humorous or swiftly moving narrative, octosyllabic couplets are a favorite. Blank verse, because of its flexibility and the opportunity which it provides for widely varied effects, is perhaps the most extensively used form. Of stanzaic forms, the Spenserian stanza has been most popular, with the rime royal also found useful. Besides these generalized forms, however, two important special forms of narrative verse may be distinguished. These are the ballad and the epic.

The **ballad** represents the simplest and most primitive attempt to tell a story in verse. Metrically it uses the simplest of all rhythms, namely, the seven-foot meter of doggerel. This meter may appear as a four-line stanza of alternating tetrameter and trimeter (the so-called "ballad stanza") with rhyme either alternate or only in the even lines, or else written in the form of seven-foot rhymed couplets. In either case the effect is the same. Occasionally the meter is slightly varied; often it is elaborated by the use of one or more refrains.

The ballad is essentially primitive in quality and characteristics. It tells a straightforward story of fighting and valorous deeds, of the emergencies and tragedies of a hard and primitive life, and of the misfortunes of unhappy love. Occasionally there is a lighter tone of homely humor, and more often there is a morbid preoccupation with the supernatural and macabre. Simple, objective, and direct, with little conscious ornamentation, the ballad is at the same time vivid and vigorous, varying in mood from grim realism to sentimental, but determined sadness. As a rule, it couples the use of conventionalized descriptive epithets and phrases with a predilection for stereotyped symbols and magical numbers. Perhaps its most characteristic feature is suspense maintained by incremental development to a surprise climax. Here the effect is often aided by the use of dialogue, dramatic colloquy, and refrain. Understatement, indirection, and irony are among its most characteristic devices.

Two kinds of ballads are ordinarily recognized. The **folk ballad** is the true primitive ballad. As its name indicates it is impersonal and communal in origin. Because of its origin in primitive society, it establishes the peculiar qualities of the ballad as outlined above. The **literary ballad** is a sophisticated imitation of the folk ballad. In general it attempts to recapture the technique and spirit of the primitive ballad, but as a rule is more self-conscious, personal, and artistically embellished than its model. Often it is more concerned with philosophical and ethical connotation than the folk ballad, wherein such considerations, if present at all, are no more than dimly implied. Such ballads as *Chevy Chase, Sir Patrick Spens, Edward,* the Robin Hood ballads, and the notorious *Frankie and Johnny* are folk ballads. Among literary ballads may be mentioned Scott's *Lochinvar,* Keats's *La Belle Dame sans Merci,* Coleridge's *Rime of the Ancient Mariner,* and Longfellow's *Wreck of the Hesperus.*

The **epic** is a long narrative poem of ambitious scope, which in verse of noble dignity sets forth the life and deeds of gods and heroic mortals of an ancient and mythical past as a reflection of national or racial ideals. Like the ballad, the epic is of primitive origin. Indeed, originally it grew out of popular ballads and lays preserved by word of mouth, constantly altering, and gradually by accretion crystallizing into the final epic form. Like the ballad, the epic is of two kinds: the popular or primitive epic, and the literary epic.

The **popular epic** is a folk heritage, a general repository of racial memory and ideals, preserved and formed as described above. Many races possess such an epic synthesis of the common past. In all, the general qualities are the same although the details of outward form may vary somewhat. The distinguishing feature of the popular epic is that it is the objective portrayal of a race or nation by itself, set down or perhaps integrated by a scribe or poet, but in no sense consciously created or materially modified by an individual genius. The only surviving example of such an English epic is *Beowulf.*

The **literary epic** is a conscious and sophisticated imitation of the popular epic. The resultant form of the epic depends upon the model imitated. Thus there is considerable difference between Longfellow's literary epic *Hiawatha* and Milton's *Paradise Lost.* The conventional form of the epic, however, has been modeled after that of the Homeric popular epics, *The Iliad* and *The Odyssey.* The authority of Virgil's *Æneid,* which is a conscious literary imitation of the Homeric poems, did much to standardize the epic form throughout Europe. Milton's *Paradise Lost* is the best English example of the conventional literary epic.

The following are the most important features of the conventional epic, particularly as regards form. It is the story of a national or racial hero, and of his deeds among gods and heroes of a mythical past. Structurally, the story is presented in three parts or movements. The first begins *in medias res,* at that point in the story which prepares for the climax; the second pauses just before the climax to recapitulate preceding events in the form of a narrative; the third resumes the story at the point of pause and includes the climax and dénouement. Gods are presented as mingling with and guiding mortals and often motivating their fortunes. Scenes are alternated between earth and heaven. Narrative and description are interspersed with dramatic dialogue. Important stages in the development of the story are marked by invocations. Enumerations of combatants, descriptions of councils, mechanical processes and games, allegorical episodes and visions are introduced as conventional embellishments. And, finally, important historical events subsequent to the action of the epic are illuminated in terms of a prophecy. In English the verse is usually blank verse, which strives for a lofty and sustained dignity and magnificence.

The elaborate machinery of the epic is admirably adapted to imposing effects on lofty themes. But when the subject is the reverse, the discrepancy between that subject and the elaborate machinery reduces all to absurdity. Thus was begotten the mock epic. The **mock epic** is a poem of variable length which treats a trivial subject with all the pomp and circumstance of epic machinery. Its aim is the ludicrous, often coupled with burlesque or satire. Pope's *The Rape of the Lock* is the most famous mock epic in English.

DRAMATIC VERSE

About dramatic verse little need be said. In general it is merely verse used as the medium of dialogue in poetic drama. In English drama the usual form is blank verse. Unquestionably the best examples are to be found in Shakespeare's plays. In another sense, dramatic verse is that kind of verse which presents its subject with the aid of certain of those dramatic methods discussed in the preceding chapter. The one specialized form which may be mentioned is the dramatic monologue.

The **dramatic monologue,** as a verse form, is a poem which endeavors to present dramatically a significant situation or incident exclusively through the speech of one of the characters. The circumstances, it should be observed, are not described or narrated by the speaker. His speech is a purely dramatic one addressed to other characters who are silent but presumably present. The personalities of the characters, the general setting, such action as occurs, and the development and revelation of the situation are suggested or implied by the words of the speaker. Examples may be found in such monologues of Browning as *Andrea del Sarto, My Last Duchess, Fra Lippo Lippi,* and *Soliloquy of the Spanish Cloister.*

LYRICAL VERSE

Of all poetic types lyrical verse is perhaps the most common, as well as the richest in resources and development. Lyrical verse is that kind of verse most intimately associated with the qualities and effects of music. Often it consists of lines actually to be sung to a musical accompaniment; but even when not designed for specific musical accompaniment, its lilt and tonal qualities are suggestive of melody and at times of harmony.

Lyrical verse is exceedingly varied in character, but in general may be said to fall into two classes. These can best be differentiated in terms of their origin. Ancient Greek poetry distinguished two kinds of lyric verse, depending upon the nature of the musical accompaniment. One was song, either individual or choral, which was accompanied by the lyre, and thus known as lyric. In general, such verse attempted no more than the expression of a mood, attitude, or emotion in song. A second kind was designed for recitation to the accompaniment of a flute, and was felt to be appropriate to more personal feeling and meditation. This kind of verse was known as elegiac verse.

Although much adapted and blended, these two strains may still be detected in modern lyrical poetry. There is what is often called the "pure lyric," the song, the hymn, which endeavors to do no more than give lyrical expression to a mood or emotion. It is usually simple, direct, personal and fluent, with overtones of music for the ear. Such are the songs of Shakespeare and Burns, and many of the lyrics of Shelley, Tennyson and Swinburne.

More common, however, is the elegiac strain. Not only does this appear in the elegy proper, but it has also produced a large volume of lyrical poetry which is predominantly meditative in character. In such lyrical verse the music is muted, thought interprets emotion, and the voice is of the soul communing with itself. Of this nature are Milton's *L'Allegro* and *Il Penseroso*, Wordsworth's *The Solitary Reaper*, Keats's *Ode to a Nightingale*, Tennyson's *Crossing the Bar*, Thompson's *The Hound of Heaven*, and the great majority of contemporary lyrics.

The forms of English lyrical poetry are as varied as the caprices of the poets. Many of the simpler stanza forms recur, but often combined and adapted into new variations. These it is profitless to codify. Such arbitrary forms as occur are of foreign origin and owe their existence to imitation. Of these there are three important lyric importations: the elegy, the ode, and the sonnet.

The **elegy** is a poem devoted to a sober meditation upon the circumstances and signification of death. It is distinguished not so much by its actual form as by the nature and ordering of its subject matter and by the purpose to which it is adapted. As to purpose, the elegy is usually designed to celebrate the death of a specific individual, although occasionally it may be prompted by any physical evidences of death. With respect to subject matter, it should be noted that the elegy is not merely a poem of lamentation. It is a philosophical meditation occasioned by death. As such it is to be distinguished from the **lament,** which is a mere expression of grief, and from the **threnody,** which is a somber contemplation of the facts or implications of death or dissolution. The elegy merely takes the subject of death as a point of departure, as a sort of theme upon which it plays variations. The ordering of these variations is largely conventional, and from this conventional ordering arises such form as the elegy possesses.

Structurally the elegy consists of three major parts or movements: the lamentation, the philosophical disquisition, and the consolation. The lamentation introduces the specific subject of the elegy, details the circumstances of the occasion, and proclaims the grief of man and nature. A recognition of the ironic brevity of life and of the frustrations caused by death leads to a philosophical disquisition on the meaning of life and death, or any subject suggested by the career of the one celebrated in the elegy. The result of this disquisition is the affirmation of a philosophical belief, which serves as the basis of the consolation with which the elegy normally concludes. The form, with certain other conventional embellishments, may be observed in Milton's *Lycidas*. Other famous English elegies are Gray's *Elegy Written in a Country Churchyard* and Shelley's *Adonais*.

The **ode,** to quote Edmund Gosse, is "any strain of enthusiastic and exalted lyrical verse directed to a fixed purpose and dealing progressively with one dignified theme." Its distinguishing characteristics are its occasional nature (that is, its origin in, and dedication to, a special occasion), its formal and dignified manner, elevated tone, choice language, and elaborate technique. It derives from the poetry of ancient Greece and Rome; and, following this derivation, appears in English in three forms, known respectively as the stanzaic, the regular, and the irregular ode.

The **stanzaic ode** comes into English by way of an

imitation of the Latin poet Horace, and for that reason
is often called the Horatian ode. While displaying the
characteristics of the ode noted above, it is particularly
marked by a uniform stanzaic structure. These stanzas
may be short and simple, as in Collins's *Ode to Evening,*
or complex and elaborate, as in Keats's *Ode to a Nightingale.* Other famous stanzaic odes are Shelley's *To a
Skylark,* Wordsworth's *Ode to Duty,* Keats's *Ode on a
Grecian Urn,* and Coleridge's *Ode to France.*

The **regular ode** is derived especially from the Greek
poet Pindar, and thus is frequently known as the Pindaric
ode. It is an intricate form composed of several divisions,
each of which consists of three parts or movements known
respectively as the strophe, antistrophe, and epode. Originally these three parts corresponded to the movements of
the chorus which sang the ode. The chorus moved to
one side during the strophe, retraced its steps with the
antistrophe, and sang the epode standing still. For this
reason, whatever the details of technical structure, the
strophe and antistrophe correspond in form while the
epode usually differs from both. The rhythmic patterns
of the three parts are usually complex, and strophic rather
than stanzaic in development. There is considerable
variety in the length of lines and, in English, in the
arrangement of rhymes as well. Although the true Pindaric ode is rare in English, excellent examples are found
in Gray's two odes, *The Bard* and *The Progress of
Poesy.*

The **irregular ode** is the common English substitute
for the more exacting Pindaric ode. Originated during

the seventeenth century, through a misunderstanding of the Pindaric technique, it rapidly usurped the place of its model. The irregular ode, as its name implies, is an ode of strophic development, which consists of an indeterminate number of strophes designed according to the metrical caprice of the poet and obeying no law but the poet's taste. Skilfully constructed, it has been an impressive vehicle of lofty poetic utterance. More often it has degenerated to the sprawling rodomontade of the uninspired poetaster. Among the great examples of the irregular ode are Dryden's *Alexander's Feast,* Wordsworth's *Ode on the Intimations of Immortality,* William Vaughn Moody's *Ode in Time of Hesitation,* and Francis Thompson's *The Hound of Heaven.*

The **sonnet,** like the ode, is a foreign importation, and is to the ode as a cameo to a monument. Borrowed from Italy during the sixteenth century, it is a lyrical form with rigorous laws which afford a challenge to the skill and craftsmanship of the painstaking artist. The sonnet is a fourteen-line iambic pentameter poem devoted to the sustained, unified, and complete expression of a single idea, mood, attitude, or impression. At its best it is marked by especially choice and pregnant language, ease, lucidity, and beauty, perfection of style, and its own peculiar flow and ebb of emotion and rhythm. In English usage two forms of the sonnet may be distinguished: the Italian sonnet, and the so-called Shakespearean sonnet.

The **Italian** or **Petrarchan sonnet** is in English an imitation of the sonnet form popularized by the Italian poet Petrarch. It consists of two quatrains rhymed on but two sounds, thus: *a b b a a b b a,* and two tercets usually rhymed either *c d e c d e* or *c d c d c d.* Conventionally there is a pause in the rhythm and sense, as well as in the structural movement of the poem, at the end of each quatrain and tercet. In practice, however, these pauses, as well as the rhyme scheme, have been varied by different poets. The regular development of the sonnet follows a conventional pattern. In the first quatrain is set forth a subject or proposition. In the second this proposition is clarified and reënforced by restatement in different terms, amplification, or illustration. The first tercet either makes particular application of that which has been set forth in the preceding lines or reflects significantly upon it. Finally, the last tercet draws all to a conclusion and illuminates it with the poet's individual interpretation. Among English writers of the sonnet there is a tendency to distinguish the first eight lines (the octave) from the last six (the sestet), to balance one against the other, and to make the sestet in effect an antiphonal response to the octave. In either case, however, a pointed conclusion, epigrammatic in effect, is avoided in the concluding lines. The proper effect should be one which gives to both meaning and rhythm a sense of subsidence from climax to final resolution. Keats's sonnet *On First Looking into Chapman's Homer* is a reasonably correct example of the Italian form.

> Much have I travell'd in the realms of gold
>> And many goodly states and kingdoms seen;
>> Round many western islands have I been
> Which bards in fealty to Apollo hold.

Oft of one wide expanse had I been told
  That deep-brow'd Homer ruled as his demesne;
  Yet did I never breathe its pure serene
Till I heard Chapman speak out loud and bold:

Then felt I like some watcher of the skies
  When a new planet swims into his ken;
Or like stout Cortez when with eagle eyes
  He stared at the Pacific—and all his men
Look'd at each other with a wild surmise—
  Silent upon a peak in Darien.

The **English** or **Shakespearean sonnet** is a modification and simplification of the Italian sonnet adopted, but not invented, by Shakespeare, and subsequently used by many poets. It consists of three alternately rhymed quatrains and a concluding couplet, the rhyme scheme being *a b a b c d c d e f e f g g*. It will be seen at once that this arrangement departs from the balanced form of the Italian sonnet. Structurally, the Shakespearean sonnet develops its idea through three cumulative stages corresponding to the three quatrains. The idea is then summed up and applied in the couplet, which as a consequence is often epigrammatic in effect. A variation of the Shakespearean form, which differs only in that the quatrains are interlocked by rhyme (*a b a b b c b c c d c d e e*) is known as the **Spenserian sonnet** because of its use by the poet Edmund Spenser.

When to the sessions of sweet silent thought
I summon up remembrance of things past,
I sigh the lack of many a thing I sought,
And with old woes new wail my dear time's waste.
Then can I drown an eye, unused to flow,

For precious friends hid in death's dateless night,
And weep afresh love's long since canceled woe,
And moan the expense of many a vanished sight—
Then can I grieve at grievances foregone,
And heavily from woe to woe tell o'er
The sad account of fore-bemoanèd moan,
Which I new pay as if not paid before.
　　But if the while I think on thee, dear friend,
　　All losses are restored and sorrows end.
　　　　　　　　　(Shakespeare, *Sonnet xxx*)

So many sonnets have been written by such a variety
of poets that it is scarcely profitable to single out special
examples. Very few poets, indeed, have resisted the sonnet
lure. But among the great English writers of the sonnet
may be mentioned Shakespeare, Spenser, Sidney, Milton,
Wordsworth, Keats, Elizabeth Barrett Browning, and
Dante Gabriel Rossetti. Although the two kinds of sonnet
mentioned above constitute the fundamental patterns of
all sonnets, it must be understood that the form has been
submitted to much experimentation and consequently
shows considerable variation in minor details. Moreover,
sonnets are frequently connected by a common theme and
thus become actually parts of a larger development and
unity. A group of sonnets so linked together is known as
a **sonnet sequence.** Some of the more famous sonnet
sequences are Shakespeare's one hundred and fifty-four
Sonnets, Spenser's *Amoretti,* Sidney's *Astrophel and
Stella,* E. B. Browning's *Sonnets from the Portuguese,*
and Rossetti's *The House of Life.*

DIDACTIC VERSE

To speak of didactic verse as a type of poetry is perhaps a bit misleading. For, even more than the types just discussed, didactic verse is not a thing apart, but may appear, and usually does, in close conjunction with other types. Indeed, verse is didactic more in spirit and intent than in kind.

Didactic verse, as its name implies, is verse directed to the end of instruction or discussion. Often its purpose is overt moral preachment or exhortation. In a sense it is verse devoted to the uses of the essay. Its appeal is to the head rather than to the heart. Its stylistic virtues are precision and pungency of expression, often with the trenchancy of epigram. Although it may make use of any verse technique, it often appears in the form of blank verse or the heroic couplet.

However varied may be the expression of didacticism in poetry, there are several verse forms with which it is often identified. Most general in nature is the **verse essay,** which may be philosophical, as Pope's *Essay on Man;* or scientific, as Erasmus Darwin's *Botanic Garden;* or economic, as Goldsmith's *Deserted Village;* or critical, as Pope's *Essay on Criticism.* Sometimes the essay is cast in the form of a letter, and is thus known as a **verse epistle.** Such are Browning's *Epistle of Karshish, the Arab Physician* and Pope's *Epistle to Dr. Arbuthnot.* Closely associated with the critical essay in verse is the verse satire. Now satire, strictly speaking, is a literary device (see p. 58); but didactic verse applied to satirical purposes is often spoken of as a **satire.** In this sense, as a form of verse, Dryden's *Absalom and Achitophel,* Pope's *Dunciad,* and Byron's *A Vision of Judgment* are among the great English satires.

There remains one of the most delightful and human of all types of verse. This may be called, for want of a more distinctive name, light verse. Light verse does not differ from other verse types in respect to its methods or forms. Indeed, it may appear as any of the foregoing types. Its real point of difference is its attitude, its manner—in short, its tone. Its true opposite is serious verse. As serious verse may be of many types and forms, so also may light verse, with a difference.

Light verse represents the Muse at play. It must not, however, for this reason be interpreted as deficient in art. In carefulness, artistry and genius, light verse is as genuinely art as the most intense and impressive poetry. As a matter of fact, it is often more fastidious in its technique than greater poetry. What distinguishes light verse is the devotion of all the artistry of verse to subjects which are usually ephemeral, humorous, or relatively trivial. Its chosen subjects are the common incidents and the pretty trifles of life. Its manner is that of well-bred culture borne with ease. Its mood may be gay, flippant and cynical, humorous, whimsical, or pleasantly sentimental. But always it is marked by ease, gracefulness, wit, and virtuosity in technique.

One of the most distinguished varieties of light verse

is **vers de société,** which might, but should not, be translated "social verse." Dedicated to the amenities of social intercourse, *vers de société* celebrates the characteristic interests, conventions, and attitudes of man as a member of society. Essentially it is a part of polite letters, with all that that implies. Its canons are those of restraint, refinement and good taste. It never engages its heart too far or too seriously. It applauds brillance, wit, elegance. In short, the Muse of *vers de société,* in the words of Don Marquis's Mehitabel, is "toujours gai" but "always the lady."

The quantity and variety of good light verse is so great, and the general quality so uniformly high, that to select illustrations is both invidious and futile. One might mention such classics as Herrick's *To the Virgins, to Make Much of Time,* Suckling's *Why So Pale and Wan, Fond Lover,* or Holmes's *The Last Leaf;* but one gains a conception of the range of light verse only from extensive reading. Among the best writers of light verse are Prior, Praed, Landor, Hood, Thackeray, O. W. Holmes, T. B. Aldrich, Andrew Lang, Austin Dobson, Eugene Field, H. C. Bunner; and in our own day, F. P. Adams, Louis Untermeyer, and Dorothy Parker. Or one may profitably turn to collections such as the three anthologies of Carolyn Wells devoted respectively to humorous verse, parody, and *vers de société.* One mood of light verse may be illustrated by the following poem of Leigh Hunt:

> Jenny kissed me when we met,
>   Jumping from the chair she sat in;

Time, you thief, who love to get
   Sweets into your list, put that in!
Say I'm weary, say I'm sad,
   Say that health and wealth have missed me,
Say I'm growing old, but add
   Jenny kissed me.

Although *vers de société* uses the greatest variety of forms, it usually prefers simplicity of structure, with a fondness for the lyrical meters and for frequency and adroitness of rhyme. Its two most familiar specialized forms are the epigram and the epitaph.

An **epigram** is a short, pungent, often witty poem of comment upon some person or incident, usually of social significance. As an example may be cited Landor's famous epigram *On His Seventy-fifth Birthday:*

I strove with none, for none was worth my strife;
   Nature I loved, and, next to Nature, Art;
I warm'd both hands before the fire of life;
   It sinks, and I am ready to depart.

The **epitaph,** which is very similar to the epigram, is also a short, pointed poem, which attempts to sum up the peculiar qualities of a person deceased. It may be touched with gentle but restrained sentiment, or it may affect a lighter mood. Of the latter sort is the Earl of Rochester's famous mock *Epitaph on Charles II:*

Here lies our Sovereign Lord the King,
   Whose word no man relies on,
Who never said a foolish thing,
   Nor ever did a wise one.

Light verse is admirably suited to parody and humorous effect. Parody has been discussed elsewhere (p. 60). **Humorous verse** includes such famous examples as Cowper's *John Gilpin's Ride,* Holmes's *The Deacon's Masterpiece,* Bret Harte's *The Heathen Chinee,* W. S. Gilbert's *Bab Ballads,* and W. L. Thayer's *Casey at the Bat.* The only important specialized form of humorous verse is the limerick.

The **limerick** has had a surprisingly wide, if rather indecorous, popularity. It is a five-line poem, of which the first, second, and fifth lines are trimeter, the third and fourth are dimeter, and the rhyme scheme is *a a b b a.* The chief art of the limerick lies in its brevity and the ingenuity of its rhymes. The following is a characteristic example:

> A wonderful bird is the pelican;
> His bill holds more than his belly can;
>   He can put in his beak
>   Enough for a week;
> I don't understand how the hell he can.

Closely akin to humorous verse is **nonsense verse.** Now nonsense verse is a genuine product of art. It has even been suggested that the true test of one's ability to appreciate poetry is the ability to appreciate nonsense verse. Indeed, it has many of the qualities of what has been called "pure poetry." Nonsense verse is verse which devotes the artistry and exquisite finish of authentic poetry to subjects which are without meaning, inconsequential, or absurd. Although usually filled with incongruities, it is not a welter of incoherence; for true non-sense verse always observes its own insane logic. The great masters of nonsense verse are Lewis Carroll, in such poems as *Jabberwocky* and *The Walrus and the Carpenter,* and Edward Lear with his limericks and *The Owl and the Pussy Cat* and *The Pobble Who Has No Toes.* The following is a brief selection from Lewis Carroll's *The Walrus and the Carpenter:*

> The sun was shining on the sea,
>   Shining with all his might:
> He did his very best to make
>   The billows smooth and bright—
> And this was odd, because it was
>   The middle of the night.
>
> The moon was shining sulkily,
>   Because she thought the sun
> Had got no business to be there
>   After the day was done—
> "It's very rude of him," she said,
>   "To come and spoil the fun!"
>
> The sea was wet as wet could be,
>   The sands were dry as dry.
> You could not see a cloud, because
>   No cloud was in the sky:
> No birds were flying overhead—
>   There were no birds to fly.

FRENCH FORMS

Of special interest in connection with light verse is a group of artificial verse forms known usually as the French forms. The French forms are a group of rigidly fixed verse patterns which, although sporadically imitated earlier, came into popularity in English verse during the last two decades of the nineteenth century. In general they owe their origin to the formal poetry of the mediæval troubadours of Provence, although they have been submitted to subsequent revision and refinement. In content and mood they may be either serious or light, but the exacting artificiality of the forms makes them particularly appropriate to the elegancies of sophistication. Their widest use in English has been in the realm of light verse.

Although there are many of these French forms, only six are of real importance in English verse. These are the ballade, the rondeau, the rondel, the triolet, the villanelle, and the sestina. A description of them follows.

The **ballade** is not to be confused with the ballad (see p. 187). The ballade is a poem consisting of three stanzas and what is known as an envoy, often written l'envoi. The meter is usually tetrameter or pentameter. Each stanza consists of eight lines rhymed *a b a b b c b C,* and the envoy of four lines rhymed *b c b C.* [Capital letters indicate lines which are repeated as a refrain.] It will be observed that the same three rhyme sounds continue throughout the poem; also that the last line of each stanza and of the envoy remains the same and serves as a refrain. Another form of the ballade (usually occurring when the meter is pentameter) uses three stanzas of ten lines, rhymed *a b a b b c c d c D,* with an envoy *c c d c D.* Three additional points may be mentioned. Except in the refrain line, no rhyme word should be re-

peated in the poem. The refrain line should sum up the
theme of the poem and serve as a natural conclusion to
each stanza in which it appears. Theoretically every ballade is addressed to a patron, as historically it actually
was. Thus the envoy, which is at once a dedication and
a peroration, conventionally begins with a formal address
to a patron, often using the terms "Prince" or "Prin-
cess." A good example of the ballade is W. E. Henley's
Ballade of Dead Actors.[19]

> Where are the passions they essayed,
> And where the tears they made to flow?
> Where the wild humours they portrayed
> For laughing worlds to see and know?
> Othello's wrath and Juliet's woe?
> Sir Peter's whims and Timon's gall?
> And Millamant and Romeo?
> Into the night go one and all.
>
> Where are the braveries, fresh or frayed?
> The plumes, the armours—friend and foe?
> The cloth of gold, the rare brocade,
> The mantles glittering to and fro?
> The pomp, the pride, the royal show?
> The cries of war and festival?
> The youth, the grace, the charm, the glow?
> Into the night go one and all.
>
> The curtain falls, the play is played:
> The Beggar packs beside the Beau;
> The Monarch troops, and troops the Maid;
> The Thunder huddles with the Snow.
> Where are the revellers high and low?

The clashing swords? The lover's call?
The dancers gleaming row on row?
Into the night go one and all.

Envoy

Prince, in one common overthrow
The Hero tumbles with the Thrall:
As dust that drives, as straws that blow,
Into the night go one and all.

Other well-known ballades are Swinburne's *Ballade of Dream Land,* Andrew Lang's *To Theocritus, in Winter,* Austin Dobson's *On a Fan,* and Rossetti's somewhat irregular translation of Villon, *The Ballade of Dead Ladies.* Swinburne's *Ballade of François Villon* is a fine example of the ten-line form.

There are two important variations of the ballade: the double, or triple, ballade; and the ballade with double refrain. The **double ballade** is the same as the ballade except that it consists of six stanzas having the same rhyme scheme and the same last line. The **triple ballade,** a rather rare tour de force, is a regular ballade of nine stanzas. Both usually omit the envoy. Examples may be found in W. E. Henley's *Double Ballade of Life and Fate* and in Alfred Noyes's *Triple Ballade of Old Japan.* The **ballade with double refrain** is a regular ballade of eight-line stanzas with two exceptions: (1) that both the fourth and eighth lines are repeated as refrains, and (2) that the fourth line of the regular stanza becomes the second line of the envoy. Thus the scheme is: three stanzas rhymed *a b a B b c b C,* with an envoy *b B c C.*

Examples are Henley's *Ballade of Youth and Age,* and
Dobson's *Ballade of Prose and Rhyme.*

The **rondeau** is a poem of thirteen lines and but two
rhymes. It is divided into three stanzas, the second and
third of which are concluded with an unrhymed refrain.
This refrain consists usually of the first half of the first
line of the poem, although occasionally it may be no
more than the first word. The meter is usually tetrameter. The rhyme scheme is *a a b b a, a a b R, a a b b a R.*
Much of the art of the poem lies in the introduction of
the refrain naturally but each time with slightly altered
meaning or emphasis. A well-known example is Austin
Dobson's *In After Days:* [20]

> In after days when grasses high
> O'er-top the stone where I shall lie,
>> Though ill or well the world adjust
>> My slender claim to honoured dust,
> I shall not question nor reply.
>
> I shall not see the morning sky;
> I shall not hear the night-wind sigh;
>> I shall be mute, as all men must
>> In after days!
>
> But yet, now living, fain were I
> That some one then should testify,
>> Saying—*He held his pen in trust*
>> *To Art, not serving shame or lust.*
> Will none? Then let my memory die
>> In after days!

[20] By permission of Oxford University Press, publishers, and Mr.
Alban Dobson.

The **rondel,** just as its name is merely an older form of the word "rondeau," is an elder variant of the rondeau form. Although there is some variation, the accepted form of the rondel is a fourteen-line poem, divided into three stanzas, in which the first two lines of the first stanza are repeated as the refrain of the last two stanzas. The rhyme scheme is either *A B b a, a b A B, a b b a A B,* or *A B a b, b a A B, a b a b A B.* To avoid monotony in repetition, the refrain of the last stanza is often reduced to but one of the two lines. An example is the following rondel by George Moore:

> The lilacs are in bloom,
>   All is that ever was,
>   And Cupids peep and pass
> Through the curtains of the room.
>
> Season of light perfume,
>   Hide all beneath thy grass.
> The lilacs are in bloom,
>   All is that ever was.
>
> Dead hopes new shapes assume;
>   Town belle and country lass
>   Forget the word "Alas,"
> For over every tomb
> The lilacs are in bloom.

[In his *Century of Roundels* the poet Swinburne developed his own variation of the rondeau. Since it has been imitated by others, a brief note on the form may be useful. The **roundel** is a poem consisting of three stanzas and two refrains rhymed *a b a R, b a b, a b a R.* The refrain consists of the first part of the first line of the poem, and usually rhymes with the *b* lines.]

The **triolet** is one of the daintiest and most graceful of verse forms, but also one of the most difficult in which to excel. It is an eight-line poem with two rhymes. Of the eight lines, one appears three times and one twice. It is in the manipulation of these repeated lines, so that they recur naturally but with varied force, that the art of the poem lies. The rhyme scheme is *A B a A a b A B*. One of the best-known triolets is Austin Dobson's *A Kiss:* [21]

> Rose kissed me to-day.
>   Will she kiss me to-morrow?
> Let it be as it may,
> Rose kissed me to-day.
> But the pleasure gives way
>   To a savour of sorrow;—
> Rose kissed me to-day,—
>   *Will* she kiss me to-morrow?

The **villanelle** is a nineteen-line poem of two rhymes. It is arranged in five tercets in such a manner that the first line of the first tercet is repeated as the last line of the second and fourth tercets, and the last line of the first tercet is repeated as the last line of the third and fifth tercets. These two repeated lines are also used as the last two lines of the final quatrain. Thus the pattern is: *A b A! a b A, a b A! a b A, a b A! a b A A!* An example which both illustrates and describes the characteristic qualities of the villanelle is the following one by Henley: [22]

[21] By permission of Oxford University Press, publishers, and Mr. Alban Dobson.
[22] By permission of Charles Scribner's Sons.

A dainty thing's the Villanelle.
　　Sly, musical, a jewel in rhyme,
It serves its purpose passing well.

A double-clappered silver bell
　　That must be made to clink in chime,
A dainty thing's the Villanelle;

And if you wish to flute a spell,
　　Or ask a meeting 'neath the lime,
It serves its purpose passing well.

You must not ask of it the swell
　　Of organs grandiose and sublime—
A dainty thing's the Villanelle;

And, filled with sweetness, as a shell
　　Is filled with sound, and launched in time,
It serves its purpose passing well.

Still fair to see and good to smell
　　As in the quaintness of its prime,
A dainty thing's the Villanelle,
It serves its purpose passing well.

The five forms just described have been the most popular and satisfactory in English imitation. One other complex form, which is more of a challenge to labor and ingenuity than to poetic genius, is the **sestina**. If for no other reason, it may be mentioned for the sake of its chief example, Kipling's *Sestina of the Tramp Royal*. The sestina is a poem of six six-line stanzas and a tercet. Its arrangement depends not upon rhyme but upon repetition of the words which end the six lines of the stanza. If these be numbered arbitrarily from one to six, the structure of the stanzas is as follows: *1 2 3 4 5 6,*

6 1 5 2 4 3, 3 6 4 1 2 5, 5 3 2 6 1 4, 4 5 1 3 6 2, 2 4 6 5 3 1. The concluding tercet uses the words numbered 2, 4, 6 to end the lines; and the words numbered 1, 3, 5 either at the beginning or in the middle of the lines. Usually there is no rhyme, but rhyme may occur on either two or three sounds.

Other exotic forms occasionally appear in English verse. Among them may be mentioned the *chant royal, kyrielle, pantoum, lai* and *virelai.* They are, however, scarcely of sufficient importance to warrant discussion here. Those who are interested may find detailed information about them in Gleeson White's useful little book, *Ballades and Rondeaus.*

INDEX